NEW
ENGLAND
FLAVOR

By Haydn S. Pearson

NEW ENGLAND FLAVOR
COUNTRY FLAVOR
SEA FLAVOR
COUNTRYMAN'S YEAR
COUNTRY FLAVOR COOKBOOK

NEW
ENGLAND
FLAVOR

MEMORIES OF
A COUNTRY BOYHOOD

By

HAYDN S. PEARSON

ILLUSTRATIONS BY LEONARD VOSBURGH

W · W · NORTON & COMPANY · INC · *New York*

COPYRIGHT © 1961 BY W. W. NORTON & COMPANY, INC.

First Edition

The author is grateful to the Boston *Herald*, the
New York *Herald Tribune*, the Philadelphia *Bulle-
tin*, and *Yankee* Magazine for permission to reprint
articles that have appeared in those publications.

Library of Congress Catalog Card No. 61-11344

All Rights Reserved
Published simultaneously in the Dominion of Canada
by George J. McLeod Limited, Toronto

PRINTED IN THE UNITED STATES OF AMERICA
FOR THE PUBLISHERS BY VAIL-BALLOU PRESS

3 4 5 6 7 8 9

To

B. E. P.

FOREWORD

"IF YOU were brought up among the hills," the old man said, "you'll always have a longing for them no matter where you go."

It was in the New Hampshire hill country and the old man and I sat on the porch of the Cape Codder house and looked across broad fields and pastures. The men were haying, and the purr of the tractor and the clickety-clack of the baler blended with the brooding heat of a perfect June day.

All around us were the hills—the beautiful blue-green hills that climbed gently from the rolling fields. A herd of Jerseys made a picture against the green of the pasture.

The old man may have been ninety; I didn't ask his age. "I know," he went on, "that my folks came up here in 1795 and made this farm out of the woods. Grandfather used to tell us children about life in the early years of the last century. He loved these mountains and the view. That's why his grandfather chose this spot.

"A group of families came up here from Connecticut. Most of them were young and had a chance to get land

7

because they had done their duty in the Revolution, and they settled here. They came up the Connecticut River Valley and then turned east and climbed into the hills.

"I wish I had lived in those early days. Life is too easy for people today. They don't appreciate what has been done for them by their ancestors. My brothers and I slept in the room that faces those hills over there, and I can remember as a boy how I looked out the window first thing in the morning. There's something about those hills over there, mister, that becomes part of your life.

"They say us New Hampshire men are hard, practical people. They make jokes about us in the papers and magazines, and we enjoy them too. But if you had been brought up here instead of in a place down south, you would know we had to be thrifty."

I had told him I was born in Farmington, New Hampshire, and had been brought up in Hancock, not too many miles south. But I had also told him I spent many years in a city near Boston.

"As a boy I began doing chores with my father and older brothers by the time I was five or six years old. Lots of things a small boy can do on a farm and I think it's wrong that boys aren't taught to work today.

"Father used to look to the hills as we went to the barn in the morning. He was a good weatherman. Not like these prophets you hear on the radio today. Father looked over to those mountains and he could tell what the weather would be. You're looking east, mister, and that's where you look for weather up here.

"Every month of the year those hills tell you something.

FOREWORD

I can't put it in words, but when you live with the hills, you get to know them. I remember when I was in school I tried to write a piece about them. I went to District Five down there in the valley. Nine grades there were in those days and I finished the ninth grade.

"We had a teacher one year who felt the same way I do about this country. He was a young fellow and he went West, I heard, and became a lawyer. He should have stayed a teacher, mister, for he knew how to teach. Had something in him beside arithmetic. He knew how to put words together so you felt things.

"Forgotten his name. But he talked about this country and its history and he knew trees and birds and he loved these hills. Some folks have to have moving pictures from a box. We've got one of 'em in the living room and the children watch the pictures. But there are pictures out here that are better. Have you ever seen these hills in October?"

"Yes," I said. "I've seen the October picture."

The old man looked at me and smiled. His hands were clasped on a stubby cane. "You know, then," he said.

"Yes," I said.

"I've lived my life here, mister, and I have had a good one. Never had much money, but my family always had plenty to eat and a warm house to live in. Mary, she was my wife, loved this land too, and we used to walk together over that pasture knoll. She is sleeping now down in the valley behind the church. I'll be with her soon.

"My children all grew up and some of them are grand-parents now. That's my oldest boy, Richard, out there on the tractor. He took over the farm and he's a good

9

farmer.

"When the hills are in a man's blood, mister, he's better off to stay here. The cities are all right for them who want them. I've been there and seen them. But I'm a hill countryman.

"It won't be long now, mister. I'm ready. I've had my life and I've spent it among these hills and it's here among them I'm going to sleep. It's hard to say what I feel, but men who like the hills will know what I mean."

I did know what the old man meant. It's hard to put New England flavor into words. Most of the time you just feel it. How do you describe the song of a brook tumbling down a pasture hillside and the music of a mountain river cascading over granite ledges? What can you say about June sunshine on buttercup-starred meadows and September haze shimmering over upland pastures? Words can't describe the furred noses of pussy willows testing crisp March air and golden fiddleheads unrolling beside peaceful country roads.

New England flavor includes rocky coastlines of Maine and sandy beaches on Cape Cod. It is old lobster houses and water-stained piers. It is a blue ocean with gentle swells and white caps dancing in the sun; and it is wild tempests when angry waves crash against the shore.

It means weathered old saphouses among patriarchal maples; green mountains silhouetted against a pale blue horizon; and river valleys with tall elms above clear water moving slowly toward the sea.

New England flavor means picture-postcard villages with maple-studded commons and tall white spires pointing to the sky. It is old roads and abandoned farmhouses, plank bridges above pebbled brooks and horse sheds behind churches. New England is old, and the patina of years gives a mellowness to a land where stone walls are patchwork-quilt stitching on the countryside.

There is another side of New England flavor. It is the remembrance of the customs, work, and play half a century ago before science lifted a magic hand and changed a nation's life.

It was in 1908 that my father brought his family to Hancock, a few miles from Greenfield where my wife Blanche and I live today. Father was graduated from Bates College and Cobb Divinity School and became a Baptist preacher. I first saw the light of day in the parsonage in Farmington, New Hampshire, on April 2, 1901.

Father held pastorates in Farmington, and in Dixfield and Gray, Maine. I have never known precisely why he gave up full-time preaching in 1908. I think it was because he found that a minister entirely dependent on his salary was unable to express himself freely. If you, by chance, are a member of a minister's family, you know what I mean. A preacher has to be careful!

Father loved country life; he loved nature. He was especially interested in apple growing and that is why he bought Glenrose Farm. The 120-acre farm had 800 old Baldwin trees, and Father intended to grow apples and preach occasionally if the opportunity offered.

I remember vividly the events of those years before World War I. I can remember when the telephone poles were set along our valley road and the magic of the brown wooden box on the wall. I remember when electric lights came to town and how happy Mother and my sisters were that they no longer had lamps and lanterns to wash and polish.

Glenrose Farm was a typical New Hampshire farm. This was an apple-growing region in those days, and just above us was a farm with 10,000 trees. Our Cape Cod farmhouse beneath its protecting maple was joined to the long barn—"continuous architecture," the city folks call it. We took part of the ell down that first summer because Father felt it was a fire hazard.

When one door closes another opens as a man goes through his life, and a few weeks after we arrived in Hancock the town's elderly minister passed to his reward. Church officials asked Father to supply the pulpit for a few weeks. The weeks stretched into months, and then

Father was asked to be the regular minister. For years he preached in the handsome white church beside the village common and above the blue water of Norway Pond. With some income from the farm, Father preached as he wished—and the chips fell, sometimes with town-reverberating emphasis.

We had cows and horses, chickens and pigs. We raised field corn and beans and a big garden. Mother jarred up tremendous quantities of fruits and vegetables. Money was scarce but we always had plenty of food.

On Sunday afternoons Father and I rambled the fields and woods, the meadows and the swamps. We climbed the mountain behind the house. It was from Father that I learned much about nature, and he gave me the interest that has made nature study a lifetime source of pleasure.

Life in those days was simple judged by modern standards. But it was a wonderful period for growing up. It was the era of fringe-topped surreys in summer and sleigh bells in winter when steel runners squeaked on the hard snow. It was the time when families gathered around a parlor organ to sing old home songs and beloved hymns; it was the era of local-talent dramatic shows, wonderful Grange suppers, and exciting debates; it was the time of traveling dog shows and Lyceum courses in winter with Swiss bell ringers, magicians, and lectures on far places of the earth.

Those were the days of home-talent minstrel shows, exuberant political rallies, and band concerts on the village common when familiar local men resembled navy admirals in their smart uniforms. It was the time when a stagecoach carried the mail to Stoddard and on over to

Keene, and we had two trains each day from Boston.

We walked to school, except in bad weather. Then I hitched Old Jerry to the democrat or the pung and put him in the village livery stable for the day. We went to church, to Sunday school, and to meeting Sunday evening. Then on Wednesday evening we went to prayer meeting.

I did all kinds of farm work. Most of it I liked, although there are more interesting tasks than picking stones, hoeing turnips, and wheeling wood into the woodshed. I milked cows and cared for the other animals. We followed the seasons with planting and cultivating, hoeing and haying, digging potatoes and stacking beans, cutting wood and getting up the ice.

I know now that I had a wonderful boyhood. I worked hard but it was probably the best of training. It is an era that is gone forever. But I'll never forget those days. Maybe if I tell you about New Hampshire the way it was when I was a boy, you'll understand what I mean by New England flavor.

HAYDN S. PEARSON
Sunny Acres
Greenfield, N.H.

NEW
ENGLAND
FLAVOR

CHAPTER ONE

THE April 2, 1908, issue of the Peterborough *Transcript* had this item in the Hancock news column. "The Rev. F. Pearson who last fall purchased the Hills place will remove his family here in the second week of April." The issue of the 16th of April states that the Pearson family had arrived.

I don't pretend to recall first impressions in order, but I can still feel the sense of spaciousness on Glenrose Farm. Looking north from the farmyard, we could see part of the village and homes on Norway Hill; behind us was a low mountain with mixed hardwoods, pines, and spruces. A clear-water brook sang down from these uplands and ran under the granite-arched road at the foot of the slope to the south of our house.

Looking to the east, it seemed like a vast unexplored

land to a seven-year-old. In front of the house, across the dirt road, was the long, upland, light-soil field. Beyond the field was our pasture, and beyond that, out of sight of the house, was the level, fertile, 30-acre meadow.

In the distance, far distance it seemed, were the mysterious mountains—the Temple Range. Today I look at those blue-green hills and know them for friendly guardians of our countryside. Half a century ago they seemed gigantic crags rising high in the sky.

Just across the road beyond the old stone wall at one end of what we called the kitchen garden stood a huge spreading apple tree. I cannot be certain, for memory can play tricks, but I have always believed this old Garden Royal was the largest apple tree I have known.

Of all the trees, the apple tree is the friendliest. It isn't gaunt and craggy like an ancient maple; it is not dignified and aloof like a patriarchal beech. It has not the majesty of a tall regal oak.

When I see a lone old apple tree in a brush-filled field today it looks friendly to me. In my rambles when I come upon an abandoned orchard on a hillside shoulder, I like to explore among the old dying trees and think of the day perhaps a century ago when a man set Northern Spies, Snow Apples, Russets, and Greenings into the spring-moist soil.

The Garden Royal at the end of our garden was a wonderful tree for a boy. The bole slanted, as is typical of many apple trees, so you could easily climb a few feet and get among the branches. In the bright sunlight there was a gray-purple hue to the bark.

The trunk, perhaps three feet in diameter, was hollowed

with the passing of many decades. Inside the trunk you could see rich black mold, the decayed heart of a tired old tree. The main limbs were huge, and many of them were hollow for several feet out from the trunk. I can remember the knotholes in the limbs and the pair of blue-birds which year after year built a nest in the limb that extended toward the road.

So far as I can remember, the Garden Royal bore a crop each year unless a late frost caught the blossoms. The Red Astrachan was our earliest apple for those first delicious pies and sauce. The August Sweet came next, and we ate those as fresh fruit or as baked apples. But ahead of the Porters and Pippins we had the Garden Royals. If picked at just the right stage of ripeness, they were crisp and juicy, fragrant and perhaps the best eating apple of all. Many a year we had ten, fifteen, or more barrels of fruit.

I don't remember the year when Father said, "I guess we'll have to cut down the Garden Royal." It may have been about 1915. Winter tempests had torn off several of the weakened, large limbs. The gaunt old tree was dying.

It wasn't a pleasant task. It always hurt Father and me to take the crosscut to an apple tree. "An apple tree is different," he would say. "I can cut pines and hemlocks, maples and oaks for our use, but I don't like to cut down what another man planted."

It was not difficult work. The huge trunk was just a shell; the main branches were hollow. We worked up the wood and hauled it to the pile in the back yard to wait for the saw.

We said good-by to the old tree. The garden was never quite the same after that. No more fragrant pink and white blossoms against the sky; no more bluebirds singing from its branches. No more could I sit in its shade, resting from weeding in the garden. Never again would we have its welcome fruit in the late summer.

There are a lot of things these days that aren't quite what they used to be when I was a boy. For example, just a little while ago I read this terse prosaic notice in the Town Warrant: "To see if the town will vote to discontinue the old Sheldon Hill road, or take any action relative thereto."

Town meeting came. Several citizens had their say about the cost of government and a few other things, and a tolerant moderator and understanding audience let them speak, even though they wandered a bit from the motion. In a small town that is the way it is. Certain voters consider it an inalienable right to speak their minds, and truth to tell, we would be disappointed if they did not.

You can figure that several of them will let off accumulated steam concerning the cost of roads and schools. Together these two items call for most of the tax money. But after the fireworks die down, the money is appropriated, and usually a little more each year. A generation and more ago we did not need too much money, and if folks would take this countryman's advice and go back to horses, top buggies, and fringe-top surreys we would all live happier. But I seem to be wandering a little bit too.

After the money-appropriation articles in the warrant were finished, the moderator read: "Article 16. To see if the town will vote to discontinue the old Sheldon Hill road, or take any action relative thereto." One voter, only a few years in town, rose and asked, "Where is the old

Sheldon Hill road?" The road agent explained. He said no one lived on the road. "I move," he said, "that the old Sheldon Hill road be discontinued." Half a dozen voices seconded the motion. "Any discussion?" asked the moderator. No one spoke. The motion was passed and not a voice was raised in opposition. No one was interested. It was just an old rutted road, with trees crowding the half-obliterated tracks. "It is a unanimous vote," the moderator said, banging his gavel.

A century ago, Sheldon Hill Road was one of the important roads of the town. Along the shoulder of the hill, there were flourishing farms and growing families. In the late 1700's, families from the Boston region came into this section. Perhaps the men came up in the fall, chose their farm sites, and established their boundaries. It was goodly country there on the sloping hillsides, darkish soil covered with white and red oaks, maples and birches.

The following spring a group of families made the pioneering journey together. Cabins and log barns were built and land cleared for a garden. In the meadows at the foot of the hill there would be hay for the cows, young stock, and oxen. Over in the next town, there was already a gristmill, so the corn and wheat could be carried on horseback to be ground for winter food.

The years passed swiftly there on the south, southeast, and southwest slopes of Sheldon Hill. Forest trees were cut and burned and fields came into being. Long lines of stone walls were built to help clear the soil and to make boundaries for mowings and pastures. Today those old walls are gray, frost-heaved, lichen-etched lines among the trees.

21

Frame houses were built when sawmills were set up. Big barns housed herds of cows and strings of oxen. Men and women with dreams in their hearts set out lilacs and peonies by kitchen doors; they planted orchards on the slopes and ran pump log lines from never-failing springs.

For two or three generations the Sheldon Hill farms thrived above the little village in the valley. Then the bright lights in the manufacturing cities on the rivers began to call. Stirring stories came back about the fertile soil of the Middle West where a man could plow all day and never would his plow point strike a stone. Most of the young folks and many of the middle-aged moved away. Trees and brush began to take back the cleared fields. Some of the buildings burned; some just became abandoned farms.

It was a single article in the Town Warrant—and the town's voters were not interested. They voted to discontinue the old road, but it is a part of New England that is gone.

I thought a lot about old roads after that town meeting. Our nation and its road system have grown together. Since man became man he has made trails to help him move easily from one place to another. In New England, after the seaboard towns were established up and down the coast, men with dreams of land and homes began trekking inland. They followed Indian trails; they explored the river valleys and climbed the mountain notches.

When a new community was established inland, the process was repeated. From the new community with its gristmill, sawmill, store and blacksmith shop, men and women went into the surrounding valleys and onto the hillsides and created farms and homes in the wilderness.

At first there were only rough trails from the outlying farms, and men and youths brought bags of corn on their shoulders to the gristmills. Then rough roads were laid out and oxcarts jerked and jolted over stumps and stones. Eventually, in meeting, a pathmaster was elected to lay out the roads of the township. The pathmasters of yester-year planned the roads to meet the needs of an ox and horse era. The roads ran from farm to farm, following the natural contours; they wound around the hills, dropped into the ravines where clear-water brooks ran down from the highlands on their way to the sea.

Back in the countryside and hilly regions, and even along stretches of the New England coast, you can still see the old roads, many of them now abandoned. There is history in the hill roads, for in pioneering days many men preferred to make their farms above the valleys. Some of them feared the "humors" that were supposed to be a part of low-lying land. There was a better chance of fending off the Indians from an upland location. And from a farmer's point of view, one could escape the early frosts of spring and fall in the uplands.

Climb an old abandoned mountain shoulder road today and you walk a path rich in history. That granite-laced cel-lar hole with the flat granite doorstep was a part of a grow-ing nation. Above the long rectangular granite-walled cel-lar was once a huge barn filled with fodder, cattle, and neatstock.

Above that smaller cellar hole was a snug farmhouse; and on that earth-floored cellar, come fall, there was food for the long winter. Over there on the brush-filled hillside you can see a few tall gaunt apple trees lifting poignant pink and white blossoms into the warm spring air.

Just an abandoned farm beside an abandoned road, says the casual traveler. But in this rocky hillside area several generations of Americans grew to manhood and womanhood. Here men and youths cleared land for crops and pasture. Here they hauled stones to line the roads and make boundaries for their fields.

Along the country road, now arched with maples and pines, birches and sumacs, boys and girls trudged to the District School at the foot of the hill. Along this dirt road, farm families drove to the village in sturdy democrats in summer and in pungs in winter. On this road, men worked with drags in the spring, and in winter rolled the snow with huge, barrel-like rollers. And a century ago, when young men and women said good-by to their parents and struck out for the brighter promises of the cities and the Middle West, it was the beginning of the end for the hill-country roads.

One of the interesting and appealing places to see old roads is in the pineland areas. Both near the coast and in certain upland areas, the old wheel tracks still starkly remind you of history. Pine trees like light sandy soil. In the pine barrens, the roads were easy to make—easy soil to grade, few stones, and a soil that dried out quickly in spring. As the ox carts and farm wagons went back and forth on the roads through the evergreens, the iron rims packed the wheel tracks hard. Any plants that started to grow were crushed. The wheel tracks became so hard that seeds rarely germinated. But in the center of the road, the scuffed and dusty horse track meant a soft mellow soil where daisies and asters, violets and grasses could find sanctuary for their roots.

Today many of the old roads through the pine woods still portray the same picture that they did decades ago. The breezes sing among the evergreen branches, and the bracing fragrance of resin fills the air. The bare wheel tracks remain, long sentences of the pages of history. The flowers and grasses blossom in the center strips. Slowly the old roads are disappearing; but some will remain for a long time—writing on the land that ties us to the past.

Last fall I was walking along one of the old roads in my neighborhood. The air was crisp and invigorating, and I walked a little farther than usual. After a while I came upon an old abandoned farm. I'd seen it many times before, of course, but today it was strangely appealing—just a small weather-beaten house sitting on a sandy knoll beside the road.

It was stark and simple in design—a Cape Codder with a central door and two windows on either side. There were two chimneys a dozen feet or so apart, and the house had one unusual feature—a door at the southeast corner.

The snaggly apple tree in the front yard was bare. The tangled limbs were a mixture of live and dead wood, and suckers were thick and tall among the branches. And behind it the house brooded in the warm sunlight of a late October day. Windows with broken panes and bare spots on the roof told the toll of years. Bricks had loosened in the capping of one of the chimneys. The blinds had long since gone.

Around the house were brush-grown fields and the trees were creeping in from the woodlands. The gray-frosted

25

heads of goldenrod and the faded blue hearts of asters blended with the amber-hued grasses cured by the sun. At one end of the house a sturdy clump of old-fashioned lilacs grew close to the foundation, and I thought that beneath the front windows I could see traces of what may have been a flower bed. Just an abandoned farmhouse beside a country road, but in that old home you can read a part of our country's history.

It may be that the records are lost and I will never know exactly when the house was built. It may have been two centuries and more ago when men came from the seacoast and made their homes here. After the first cabin was built and land cleared to grow food for the family and the farm animals, men and boys went into the woodlands in winter and got out the lumber for a frame house. In most communities, as soon as a group of families established homes around the village common and others opened up farms in the surrounding countryside, a sawmill was built and a blacksmith shop established.

In many of the old homes and barns, hand-hewn timbers were used because labor was plentiful and all the work could be done right on the farm. But boards were commonly sawed at the mill for the siding, roof, and floors. Nails were handmade by the blacksmith and in early days were very expensive. That is why in so many barns and houses wooden trunnels were used to tie the framework together.

Except for the glass in the windows and the bricks for the chimney, a man and his sons provided the building materials from the farm. The granite foundation stones came from the fields; the foundation for the chimney was laid up with flat granite rocks. Chances are that the chimney bricks came from a local kiln where bricks were molded of local clay and baked hard in a wood-fired kiln.

Was this house built in 1760, over two hundred years ago? Six generations ago was this home filled with the laughter of children? Was the earth-floored cellar stored two centuries ago this autumn with potatoes and turnips? In those attic rooms were there bunches of dried herbs hanging from pegs in the rafters? In the kitchen with its spacious fireplace, brick oven, and ash pit below, was there the fragrance of freshly baked loaves of whole-wheat bread and satisfying odors from a venison stew bubbling in a big iron pot hanging from the crane? Perhaps in the evening a mother sat at the spinning wheel and a father whittled pieces of equipment for home and farm from straight-grained chunks of pine or ash.

I do not know the story. But now this abandoned farm sits patiently through the turning years. The decades come and go and time takes its inevitable toll. The world rushes on and people seem to feel it necessary to rush through their days. But some of the abandoned homes on the hill-sides will remain for a long time—memorials to the men and women who fought a good fight and dreamed good dreams.

Two centuries ago pioneers throughout the Northeast were building stone walls with the rocks that lay thick on the land and in the top foot or two of soil. Tens of thousands of miles were built as settlers cleared land for mowings and upland pastures. A standard rule was a rod of wall a day for an ox team, two men, and a stone boat. As soon

27

as pathmasters laid out the curving roads that followed natural contours from farm to farm, stone walls were often built on either side of the road. Walls were built around lush meadows to keep cattle out; walls lined the cattle lanes from barns to pastures. Stone walls enclosed pounds and God's acres on the hillsides behind white-spired churches.

Now huge machines with massive blades are ripping up the walls that have long encircled small fields. The roaring monsters toss big boulders around as if they were pebbles; the machines nudge the rocks into piles or tip them into ravines. It means larger fields and more efficient farming operations. Even as this is going on, vast areas of land once cleared by back-breaking, plodding labor are returning to the forest from which they were wrested. You can see the old, frost-tumbled walls in the woodlands—land that once was pasture or grain field.

"Making land" is a term I no longer hear. But in 1910 when I was a boy, I can remember Father saying on a late fall Saturday, "Hitch Old Jerry to the stone boat, Haydn, and we'll make a little land."

Making land on Glenrose Farm usually meant prying up rocks and hauling them away on the stone boat. I remember the area at the low end of our upland field which we cleared and which raised excellent crops of oats. I also remember some of the stumps that stood there, stumps from lumbering before we bought the farm. Digging out around those stumps and cutting off main roots was a monotonous job, and ever since I haven't been very fond of stumps. After the preliminary operations, we used the team of work horses and a long chain carefully placed around the stump to get the best leverage. I enjoyed

28

driving the team with the pulled stump and its tangled, waving roots to the pile where they would be burned.

Few persons realize that a hundred years and more ago stump pulling was an important vocation. In most rural communities one or more men were professional stump pullers. In Eric Sloane's interesting book, *The Seasons of America Past,* there is this quotation from an English writer: "The American landscape is sprinkled with stumps, like freckles on a farmer's face. Some dig them out and use them as ugly stump fences, but others leave them in place, where they will probably stay for the next century, and grow crops all around them."

Mr. Sloane says, "There were about 500 kinds of stump-pullers on the market in the 1800's, and stump-pulling became a common American profession. Stump-pulling was one of the few cash businesses, and at 25 cents a stump, the standard price in 1850, a man could pull from 25 to 50 stumps a day and make a most exceptional living for those days."

There is something in a man that makes him want to clear land. There is something in many of us that craves the satisfaction of working with good soil and watching things grow. I "made" a few small areas on my own farm not so long ago. I dug out rocks and took down a dozen trees. A tractor rooted out the stumps for me, and now a hundred cultivated blueberries are growing on the area.

We'll never know all the hardships that men and women of yesteryear experienced as they settled on virgin land and created homes where there had been wilderness for thousands of years. Much of the land they cleared has gone back to the forest for which it is best fitted, but it is good for a man to pause and think of those who made land long ago.

Everywhere you go in New England there are reminders of these early settlers. Do you remember the old stone bridges? Occasionally you find one—a single slab of stone spanning a brook in a meadow or a brook in an upland pasture where the water tumbles down from the highlands. The stone that serves as a bridge is wagon wide, and it rests on smaller rocks that serve as abutments. I have been told that some of these stone bridges are made of two or even three stones, but I have only seen the single-stone type.

The single-stone bridges were made by individual farmers to help them on their farms. If a man had a sugar orchard on a stony-soil upland and had to cross a brook that ran down from the highlands above, he needed a dependable crossing for the ox sled with its hogshead of collected sap. If the right-sized stones were available many farmers preferred to use the rocks rather than trees. It must have been hard work to pull some of the huge single slabs of stone in place. One wonders at the patience and ingenuity of men who built these bridges, the granite walls of great barns, and the walls of earth-floored house cellars.

In the old days, there were various ways of getting across a brook with a yoke of oxen or a team of horses. On Glenrose Farm, a brook flowed the entire length of the rectangular thirty-acre meadow. We crossed it over a stone-bottomed fording place. It may have been a century or more before we came that a farmer and his sons made the fording place. They hauled or dragged in hundreds of stones, from the size of a baseball to the size of a man's head. They brought

in enough to make a roadway across the ten-foot-wide brook. In spring-freshet time, the gray-green water boiled over the stones to a depth of a foot or more. In July—haying time in a normal season—the tops of the rocks showed. In a very dry year, the slow-moving water trickled among the stones and was barely seen.

I can remember when I was about twelve, Father asked me to haul in a few loads of small stones. "About the size of a good Baldwin apple," he told me. I loaded the cart at a gravel bank on the north side of the orchard, or went to the big stone pile at the low end of our upland field. Old Jerry and I carted them to the brook, and bare-footed, I spread them on the fording place wherever I saw a gap between larger stones that needed filling in.

And now almost half a century later, I can still feel the lurching of the load of hay as we crossed the brook. I can still feel the bone-jarring bumping of the horse rake as the big metal wheels banged over the rough passage.

Many of the early bridges were made of oak, chestnut, or hard maple logs, flattened on top, for stringers. The other logs were adzed flat to lay on the stringers. On the side roads of New England, you can still find many of these plank bridges—the abutments still firm and trim, the old planks weathered and splintered.

Do you remember how the weather-grayed planks rattled when you hit the bridge at a good clip behind a fast-stepping Morgan? The wagon struck the first loose plank and set off a continuous reverberating roar as you crossed the bridge. Jugs of cream bounced and you could feel the bridge vibrations through the worn-out wagon springs and upholstery of the battered front seat.

No one knows the number of humble utilitarian bridges that have been built in this nation. They are true functional architecture and in their plain usefulness represent the basic qualities of the men who built them. The early roads meandered casually beside meadow streams and wandered around the shoulders of low hills. At first, the brooks were forded. Sometimes men tossed loads of rocks into the stream beds, as they had at Glenrose Farm. But a problem remained, for in the time of spring freshets, water ran high and fast between the banks.

Thus plank bridges came into being. On a given day, men and boys gathered with ox teams, stone boats, and crowbars. Huge granite rocks were placed in position for abutments; the stringers were stretched across, and the three- or four-inch hardwood planks were set in place. Sometimes railings were built along the sides; sometimes a log was rolled into position at each end of the bridge. And when the bridge was built, farm families knew they could get to town at any time of year.

From ten thousand hills the brooks that are born in highland springs have sung their way down stony hillsides, through peaceful woodlands and beneath the old bridges.

An old plank bridge was a fascinating spot to a twelve-year-older on his way home from District School. It was fun to explore beneath the bridge in bare feet. The abutment rocks were green and slippery with moist moss, and a boy making his way along with precarious toe and hand hold could imagine he was climbing one of the Swiss mountains illustrated in the old dog-eared geography book.

It was cool and shadowy beneath the bridge. Water bugs skittered back and forth on the surface and silver minnows

33

flashed from the rock shadows. Sometimes a jewel-sided trout lay facing upstream, gently moving its tail. A lad always watched for the famous big trout that oldtimers claimed had lived beneath the bridge for half a century. Occasionally a long, dark-colored water snake went slithering away downstream, its head held high above the water, looking like the fabled sea serpent in *Nature's Unbelievable Wonders,* the book a slick-talking salesman had sold Mother for $3.98.

Now the old plank bridges are disappearing. Steel and cement are the materials needed for modern traffic to speed man and his products from place to place. But some of the stained, battered bridges will remain for years to come. The splintered path will remain to remind us of the days when iron-shod horses trotted across the planks and the rattling roar sounded like thunder to a boy underneath.

Country dirt roads varied greatly half a century ago. Today even fifth-class roads are likely to get a coat of gravel in rural areas as a result of state funds to supplement money raised by a town. But in the days when women wore rats in their hair and men kept their chins up because of high stiff collars, country roads had individuality and personality. Each road to town from outlying farms had its famous holes in mud times, stretches of soft sand that developed deep ruts, and hills where thank-you-ma'ams offered welcome rest spots to a blowing team.

Split-log road drags were used to get dirt roads in shape for the season. Each road agent in town had one; it was made of a log, perhaps a foot in diameter, split down the middle. The two halves were fastened together by two-by-fours which were set in holes cut in the logs. The vertical side of each log faced the front. The two-by-fours were usually four or five feet long and a couple of planks were bolted onto the cross timbers. It was on these planks that the driver stood, often accompanied by two or three small fry of the neighborhood.

A country road in spring, just after the mud season, was in need of attention. There were places in the clay stretches where the ruts were a foot or more deep. There were mud holes that were a couple feet deep, and everyone who used the road knew about them and circled around them. I can remember places where men had trouble hauling home a load of grain and had taken big rocks from the stone wall beside the road and tossed them into the soft spots. On the hills, spring freshets washed deep gullies and undercut the roadsides.

The split-log drag was an efficient tool. You started at the outside edge of the road, and the split-log halves which were set on a bias pulled soil, leaves, stones, and debris toward the center. Back and forth along a section of road went the road agent with his team of big work horses. Each trip along each side meant that a mass of material was scraped toward the center of the road. The basic idea was that if you rounded up the center of the road in good shape, when it rained the water would run off to the sides.

It was hard work dragging a road. When I was fourteen or so, I remember that I got 15 cents an hour for going along with a rake and getting rid of the larger stones. The really big stones I had to give a hearty heave to send them off to the sides. There was even more work on the hills, because we usually had to rebuild the thank-you-ma'ams.

35

A country road in the wintertime is another thing again. You haven't really lived until you've sat on the wooden platform atop a big snow roller and held the lines over four or six willing horses. Bundled in a mackinaw and wearing arctics and felt leggings, I used to ride the snow roller with Mr. Adams, the road agent in charge of our section of town.

It was a beautiful winter day. The big storm had blown itself out and a foot of fluffy dry snow had painted a sparkling picture on the countryside. The sun circled in a clear blue sky and the stocking caps on the fence posts glistened in the slanting rays. The mountains across the valley were silhouetted against the pale blue horizon. A snow storm was a welcome interlude to a fourteen-year-older. It meant District School was called off for a couple of days while the roads were rolled, and farm boys could earn a dollar a day.

A light dry snow was the easiest to handle. The huge roller, looking like two big slatted barrels, went groaning and creaking along the country road, pressing down the snow. A dry snow with a high wind was second best in my opinion, for it meant plenty of shoveling in the drifted spots, and it might take three days to get the roads in shape. The snow wasn't heavy and I didn't mind a little work.

Best of all, from an economic viewpoint with mail order time coming up and a lad's finances slender, was a wet heavy snow. Then the horses had to stop frequently and I had to knock the snowballs from their hooves. That meant a long, slow-moving, and monotonous session, but an extra workday meant an extra dollar.

In the winter, road work was pretty simple. Sleighs, cutters, pungs, and farm sleds needed only two tracks. The shafts on single-horse sleighs were offset so that a horse traveled directly ahead of the left runner. In double-runner outfits each horse went in front of a runner. Naturally this system of two-track traveling had its drawback. If a lad were driving the snappy Morgan in the pung to the village and met another pung, each had to turn out and the outside runner dropped into soft snow. More than once I felt that outside runner sink down and I was flipped over into the ditch.

No one knows who invented the snow roller and when the first one was made. Some claim it is a progeny of the great hogsheads of tobacco that were rolled down through the White Mountain notches. The rollers came in various sizes, but basically all conformed to the same engineering principles. Some were small and easily handled by one team; some were eight feet high, of large diameter, and needed six or eight big horses. The two barrel-like rollers worked on a long axle that went through the centers of both barrels. A framework was built around the rollers. Usually a small platform on top was the driver's seat, but some of the smaller-diameter rollers had a driver's seat fastened to the framework just behind the horses. I have seen a few rollers with a platform across the entire top of the two rollers and a box with a board across it for the driver on the platform.

After a big storm, Mr. Adams called two or three farmers along the road and arranged for the horse power. I can remember taking Old Jerry and Charlie and riding one and leading the other over to his farm. Then we hitched them up to the roller and started out on the road. At each farmhouse we made a circle of the yard and perhaps took a turn around one end of a barn. Womenfolks came out with hot doughnuts and coffee, cake and turnovers, so that by the time the bell in the village steeple tolled noon, I was so full I barely touched the food in the five-pound lard pail that Mother packed for my lunch.

It was good to work on the hills and look across the valley with its line of vaselike elms; good to see the folks at the farms and to exchange banter and jibes, even when they asked Mr. Adams if the taxpayers were getting their money's worth from that lazy boy he had hired.

Some folks have the erroneous idea that there are only four seasons, but if you have ever lived on a dirt road, you know there is a fifth season sandwiched between winter and spring—mud time.

Mud time varies from year to year, depending upon the severity of the winter, the amount of snow, lateness of the winter season, April winds and sunshine, and the type of soil that forms the road foundation. If plenty of snow covers the ground from November to April, the frost does not go down too deeply. Then if April has wind plus sun and high temperatures, the mud season is over quickly. But you can never tell in the country, and a farmer always gets ready for mud time just in case. He makes sure he has a good supply of grain, kerosene, paint for the farm wagons, matches, and tobacco. His wife checks her supply of flour, sugar, salt, coffee, and tea.

On most dirt roads, between a farm and a nearby hard road, or between a farm and the village, there were usually several well-known mud holes. There were two beauties between Glenrose Farm and the village the spring that I finally persuaded my father that it would be safe to drive the Buick to town.

The Buick, one of the old-time four-cylinder models, was Father's pride and joy. "Better take the horse, Haydn," he said. "It will be a lot safer. Those mud holes are treacherous."

It would have been safer. No question of that. With a horse and democrat you always got through. The fence was taken down each spring along these locally famous spots, so you could drive around the mud hole along the edge of the field. But I had confidence. Besides, there had been a good sharp frost the previous night. "I'll skim right across those holes," I told Father.

The first half mile along a sandy upland was easy. Then I dipped down to a plank bridge and started up the clay stretch toward Charlie Sheldon's. I came to the treacherous spot. It looked firmly crusted. I picked up a little speed for a safety margin. I came to the mud hole. The car broke through the crust. I stopped—very suddenly—and settled down to the running boards.

Charlie Sheldon was hitching his team to a wagon in the yard. He unhitched and came down to me with the evener and whiffletree dangling along behind the big team. He didn't scold; he didn't even smile. He pulled the Buick out of the mud hole, took it into his yard and turned it around. Then, without even bothering to unhitch, he drove his team down the road again and pulled the Buick back through the mud hole. When it was on the other side of the hole, he unhitched. "Be kinder soft here for another week, Haydn," he said.

As luck would have it, Father was in the yard when I reached home. The Buick, spotless when I started, was covered with mud. I could see Father's quiet, rather sad smile as I drove up to the garage space in the ell. He never said a word, just smiled that smile and went on to the barn. I changed my clothes, got buckets and cloths and washed the car.

CHAPTER TWO

THE big poster in the General Store proclaimed in eye-arresting type: "Genuine Old-Fashioned Country Auction." It was a mellow sunny fall Saturday, and Blanche and I decided we might as well go over and take a look.

The auctioneer was in good form. He had a large audience and the bidding was lively. It was, indeed, a genuine old-fashioned country auction and people were eager to bid for the items. The crowd, most of them summer folks up for the week-end, was in high spirits. Good fun, good sport to bid and get something for their country homes.

The old hillside farm family had run out; nephews and nieces had decided that Aunt Mary Pettingill could no longer live alone on Mountain View Farm. For a century and a half, a Pettingill had farmed the sidehill fields. For a century and a half, Pettingills had sent boys to fight their country's wars. For a century and a half, Pettingills had been selectmen, school trustees, and leading citizens of the

41

New Hampshire hill town. Aunt Mary sat by herself—to one side. Old friends came to speak to her and moved along. What does one say? Her husband had died several years before. Their only son had been killed in France during the First World War. He had answered his country's call.

"Look at this Boston rocker!" the auctioneer shouted. "It's the real thing. You city fellows get all tired out raising petunias and sweet peas. This is what you need to get rested. Better to rock yourself than get one of them newfangled contraptions that shake you to pieces. What am I offered? A dollar! A dollar I've got. Two I've got. Who'll make it five? Three? Thank you, sir. Four I've got. Now go to five, go to five, go to five. Five I've got and who'll make it six? Five I've got and who'll make it six? Are you done? All done? Sold for five dollars to the gentleman in the snappy plaid shorts. Now look at this cherry drop-leaf table."

I looked at Aunt Mary—Aunt Mary sitting alone in a straight-backed chair, and I saw her lips tremble. I wonder what she was thinking. Was she thinking of those long ago years when John was a baby and she cuddled him in her arms and rocked him in that chair before the gleaming kitchen stove.

"Who'll start it for ten dollars? It's a beauty. Two drop leaves and in perfect condition. Shows a little wear on the top, but you can get it refinished. Do it yourself. Only takes a little elbow grease. Ten dollars I've got; now make it twenty. Who'll make it twenty? Fifteen? Thank you, sir. Now I've got twenty. All done? Going, going, gone for twenty dollars to the lady in the pink shirt."

Shows a little wear on the top! Aunt Mary looked across

the fields to her beloved mountains looming against the southwestern sky. A little worn! Her father gave her that table when she came to Mountain View Farm as Abner's bride. For almost sixty years she had made cakes and pies, biscuits and cookies on that table. Twice a week for half a century, until Abner went to his rest behind the church on the common, she had set her bread to rise on that table.

"And look at this old kerosene lamp!" cried the auctioneer. "It's a good one. Wire it up and you have real light to read your novels by."

Aunt Mary looked around. Mostly strangers. Old friends? Most of them were gone now. I saw a strange little smile come to her lips as she thought of the fall and winter evenings when that tall lamp with its shade had stood on the table in the living room. Abner sat at one side of the table, reading the city paper, the town weekly, and his farm journals. She read her woman's magazine, sewed for Abner and John, knitted socks and wristers. And every Saturday night over the years she and Abner had read the Bible selection for the Sunday school lesson in the golden glow of the light.

Blanche and I exchanged a few words with Aunt Mary before we left. She told us she was well provided for—her nephew was taking care of that—but she said she was sad to see all the old things go. "Times have changed," she said, "but I've still got my memories. I guess they can't auction those off."

My memories don't go back as far as Aunt Mary's, but I've got quite a few of them. For instance, I remember the old sap buckets with one long stave with a hole in it that fitted over a nail or spout on a tree. They are antiques nowadays, and the summer folks use them for magazines or kindling wood. But when I was a boy, sap buckets were sap buckets and they were made to last.

Old-time coopers were master craftsmen. They made cider barrels, flour barrels, and barrels to hold salt pork. They fashioned milk pails, butter firkins, and several kinds of churns. And they made sap buckets. The dictionary says that a cooper is "a maker or repairer of barrels or casks," but that doesn't tell the complete story. A century and more ago the cooper was a vital cog in the rural economy. A cooper, as distinguished from a carpenter, was a crafts-man who made articles drawn together with wooden hoops. Furthermore, there were well-drawn distinctions between classes of coopers, just as there were distinctions between groups of carpenters. A man who built houses, for example, had a different rating than a man who built fine cabinets.

In general, there were two classes of coopers a century ago. The "slack" coopers made barrels and buckets that did not need to be watertight: flour barrels, salt barrels, and fruit barrels. The "tight" coopers made cider and whiskey barrels, churns, meat casks, pickle casks, milk pails, and sap buckets.

No one knows how many hundreds of thousands, per-haps millions, of sap buckets were made in New England. From all I can discover, they were made of the best easy-splitting virgin pine. You might think it would be easy to fashion a sap bucket, yet what could be more worthless than a bucket that leaked? The staves were rived with frow and maul, and both front and back of the staves showed the wood grain untouched by any tool. But the stave edges had to be beveled and jointed, and the bottoms of the staves had to fit perfectly into the groove, or chine, cut out to receive them. A century ago, a common price for these sap buckets, entirely handmade, was six cents.

An oak butter firkin is an even better example of fine cooper craftsmanship. Certain coopers in dairying regions made reputations for the excellent firkins they fashioned of white oak. The staves were commonly 33 inches in length, made from bolts, or chunks, of straight-grained white oak. The bolts were seasoned or dried for many months under cover. The finished butter tub was an object of fine craftsmanship, as well as a utilitarian affair. All that was necessary with a sap bucket was to be certain it was watertight. A butter firkin, however, was made of staves planed on both sides and was usually varnished on the outside.

The old-time cooper worked with a few tools, especially designed for their functions. Straight-grained chunks of wood, commonly white pine and cedar for softwoods, and white oak for hard, were seasoned before splitting. The cooper set a bolt on a block and split the staves with frow and maul. The frow, or froe, was a cleaving tool with the wooden handle set at a right angle to the heavy metal blade. The frow split off the staves from the block of wood. This was the riving process.

One of the most difficult phases of coopering was making the hoops that held the staves together. After the staves were rived, they were set in a framework and bound tightly with the hoops. Saplings of ash, white oak, probably alder and gray birch were commonly used. The saplings were split with a drawshave to get hoops of the desired thickness. The hoops had notches at the ends by which they were locked together. It took a practiced eye and skilled hand to cut these notches so they would fit exactly. After the saplings were split, they were soaked for a spell before the cooper took them, fitted them over a cask or barrel, measured the required length by eye, and then cut the notches. After the notched ends were snapped together, the natural drying-out process pulled the hoops tight.

I have never seen an old-time cooper make buckets or firkins. I have never watched a craftsman make cider barrels or pickle casks. But I have watched a man who turned out apple barrels by the thousands. In 1910 southern New Hampshire was famous as a region where Baldwin apples did well. Hancock had many good orchards. We had 800 Baldwin trees on Glenrose Farm; the Hayward farm, a mile above us, had 10,000 trees. Fred Johnson, on the Peterborough road, was the town cooper. His old mill was a part of my youth. I hauled many loads of white-pine logs, hemlock, and some hardwood logs to Johnson's Mill. I can recall driving Old Jerry and Charlie with a loaded sled when I was perhaps twelve years old. Father made arrangements with Mr. Johnson to unload the logs in the mill yard after I drove the team over.

Fred Johnson sawed out boards and timbers for his neighbors; he made shingles and he made apple barrels. He sawed out the staves and bottom and top ends. I don't pretend to remember all the details, but I think he set the staves in a circular framework that made a barrel of just the exact size. The staves varied in width from two or three up to four or five inches, for a guess. They were, of course, curved a bit to make the circular barrel. The hoops were sawed strips of lumber about an inch wide and perhaps a

46

quarter of an inch thick. I think Mr. Johnson put on the hoops when they were wet, but I am not sure of this. I remember when we were filling and heading the barrels in the orchard, we drove down the hoops that were above the middle bulge of the barrel. The bottom and top of the staves were grooved so the circular heads and bottoms would fit into the groove.

Over the years, I carried many loads of barrels home in the one-horse hay rack—and thereby hangs an episode that ı shall long remember. The one-horse hay rack, with its flaring sides, held perhaps thirty barrels, perhaps a few more. Father had it all figured out. The very top row of barrels was well up in the air and I rode on the top row. The load was tied on with long strong rope. One day when I was about fifteen and knew considerably more than I do now, I figured I could put on another dozen barrels or so without any trouble. Probably I'd been studying rope hitches in the Boy Scout manual. Everything went well until we started down Putnam's Hill, a short distance from the farm. All of a sudden that load of barrels disintegrated. I landed in the ditch; some of the barrels rolled down the hill. Old Jerry just stood still.

I brushed myself off, got back on, and Old Jerry and I went home with the barrels in the rack. We had to make a special trip to pick up the rest of the barrels. When Father found out what had happened, he didn't scold me— he never did. He just smiled and said, "A lazy man's load usually means more work in the end."

It was always exciting when Father said after Saturday breakfast, "Son, Belle needs a new set of shoes. Why don't

47

you hitch her to the pung and bring home a couple bags of cottonseed meal and a bag of cornmeal?"

The old ramshackle blacksmith shop sat against the hill at the south end of the long, tree-arched, village street. It was a low sprawling building, a fascinating place for boys and a stormy-day gathering place for men. It wasn't an example of good housekeeping, by any means, but Mr. Russell, elderly blacksmith, knew where everything was located. The shop was long and dingy. The floor was black and grimy, littered with hoof parings, shavings, and bits of metal. The windows were dark and dirty, covered with blotches of gray sooty cobwebs. At one side, against the wall, were the forge and anvil. At one end of the shop there was a big pile of old discarded shoes; the other end of the rectangular room was a jungle of lumber and pieces of farm equipment waiting to be repaired.

Overhead, the two-by-six cross timbers were lined with new shoes—light dainty ones for 1,000-pound roaders, and solid heavy shoes for farm work horses. At the end of the shop near the pile of rusty worn-out shoes was the massive ox sling, a framework where the half shoes were put on oxen. The ox was put in the sling, with a wide heavy belt fastened beneath him, and then raised by a windlass. One foot at a time was tied to a corner post, and the half shoes were nailed on the split hooves.

The working area for shoeing was in the middle of the shop. The old, soot-covered, bricked-up forge had seen service for a long time. Mr. Russell burned soft coal in the forge. When he used the tongs to push a shoe into the fire, he held the tongs with his right hand and operated the bellows with his left. The jets of pumped air quickly turned the mass of black to a glowing red, and Mr. Russell would pull the red shoe from the coals, hold it up, look at it, and then likely enough put it back in the fire for another few seconds.

When the shoe was red hot, he quickly laid it on the blocky, solid anvil and began pounding it with a heavy hammer. At each blow, sparks of red-orange flew high and made a graceful arch in the semigloom of the shop. The blows on the shoe echoed with loud, hollow-sounding, clanging booms. Then he turned and pushed the still-hot shoe into a half tub of black scummy water. Thick steam billowed upward, a gray cloud that disappeared among the rafters. It never seemed to me that Mr. Russell left the shoe in the water long enough.

Quickly he reached down, pulled up one of Belle's legs, fixed it between his knees, and set the shoe against her hoof. Then came the part that bothered me the most. When the hot shoe went against the horse's hoof, the hoof burned and smoked. Mr. Russell had to explain to several generations of boys that it didn't hurt the horse. "It's like your finger nail," he would say. "Don't hurt to cut your nail; don't hurt to shoe your horse."

I can still smell the burning hoof. I remember that pungent, acrid, nostril-tickling smell of smoking hoof and hot iron. Usually it took two or three fittings to get the shoe just right. That was why farmers for miles around came to Mr. Russell. He was conscientious. He used to tell us the same thing we heard from our fathers. There is only one way to do a thing, and that way is to do it right.

The shoe was heated again in the forge, shaped some more. Sometimes he pared the hoof to get the surface he

wanted. But eventually the shoe was right and fitted solidly.
He took nails from the box beside him, and with hard
sharp blows drove them through the holes in the shoes
and into the hoof. Then he snatched up a pair of nail
cutters and snipped off the ends of the protruding nails.
After he smoothed off the nail ends with a rough file, he
dropped the horse's leg with a thud, and was ready to fit
another shoe.

MEMORIES OF A COUNTRY BOYHOOD

Time was, half a century ago, when the village black-smith was an essential cog in the town's operations. He was much more than a man who shod horses. He was a carpenter and ironworker; farmers and villagers brought in wagons and sleds, plows and harnesses to be repaired. He fitted iron tires to heavy farm wagon wheels and to wheels of light-top buggies. I remember Mr. Russell well. He was in his sixties when I was about twelve; he was not a tall man, but he had broad muscular shoulders and large powerful hands. He not only shod horses and oxen, he was a master at tightening rims on a wagon wheel and he mended plows, harrows, and cultivators. If shoeing work eased up in haying, harvesting, or plowing times, he made whiffletrees to sell and got caught up on repair jobs.

The blacksmith shop was one of the best spots in town. Because Mr. Russell was a gentleman of the old school, mothers and fathers had no hesitancy about letting boys go there. Mr. Russell was a substantial citizen, a deacon in the church and a member of the school committee. He never used rough language and permitted no profanity in his shop. He liked boys and enjoyed telling them something of the history of iron. He told us that iron was known by the ancient Assyrians and was used as money by the Romans when they were in England. We learned that iron was probably discovered by accident in the ashes of a fire built close to an iron-bearing rock. He told us that horseshoes were first used about 200 B.C. and that they were made in dozens of shapes and weights.

Not very exciting, perhaps, to modern farm boys who drive powerful tractors and trucks, but it was pretty exciting to me. Now the blacksmith shops are gone; today the modern blacksmith serves a wide territory by taking his equipment on a truck directly to the farm. Each year the number of horses and mules in this country decreases, but some of us will never forget the old blacksmith shop.

I still remember the old saphouses too. I saw one just the other day on one of my walks. It was just an old broken-down building crouching among gaunt craggy sugar maples on a rock-littered south slope. The weather-furrowed boards were gray with the years, and on the north side of the house patches of thick moss painted a blended symphony of green and silver. The plank door hung by one hinge, and a few panes of broken glass reflected golden glints in the afternoon sun.

In the murky interior light, I could see the broken crumbling arch and the rusted evaporator pan, half filled with matted soggy leaves. A few broken wooden sap buckets were piled in a corner and a dilapidated half-bushel basket was filled with dark-stained spiles. On the rafter plate there was a mud-lined phoebe's nest.

It may have been a century ago when a farmer and his sons built the saphouse during brisk fall days. They laid hand-hewed sills on flat granite rocks and built an arch of granite stones. They cut wood and piled it in the lean-to shed, now fallen to the earth and returning to dark humus.

In late winter, men and boys tapped the maples that gave them sweet sap on mellow, sun-bright March days. Along the rutted roads of this grove, plodding ox teams pulled a wooden-runner sled with a hogshead waiting to be filled with sap. There were times of good sap runs when the fire beneath the evaporator was kept blazing day and night. There were sugaring-off parties on starlit March evenings when friends and neighbors gathered for sugar on snow, eggs boiled in sap, doughnuts and pickles.

Now it is no longer profitable to operate the small grove with its rough terrain. The old maples stand like patriarchs, big craggy trees with deeply furrowed bark. The maples and the saphouse have grown old together, knowing the heat of summer, the glory of autumn, the blizzards of winter, and the resurrection of spring. The old house and the old trees are time-tired now and waiting out their years.

There was a time when it was profitable for a hillside farmer to make a hundred gallons or more of syrup from his grove of three or four hundred trees. The work came at the end of winter when there was little else to do on the farm, but now in a world grown increasingly scientific, old methods are not profitable. Today sap is brought via pipeline to the house or to central collecting points. Many modern plants use oil for fuel instead of wood. Temperatures are carefully controlled and a hydrometer guarantees a certain density of product. In the old days, many a farm wife took charge of the last stages of "boiling down" and determined just when the syrup was thick enough.

As I walked on by the saphouse, I missed the sound of happy voices in the sugar grove; I missed the gray clouds of steam billowing from the door and window and the blue-gray banners of smoke spiraling from the chimney. I left the old saphouse to drowse its remaining years among the friendly maples that once gave it their life juice.

The old gristmills are gone too. But sometimes, far back in the country in a mountain valley, you come upon the ruins of an old mill. Sometimes you can see the granite-block foundation and the ruins of an old dam. Occasionally there are pieces of metal or blocks of wood lying among the bushes, vines, and old trees. The old mill pond may still have water in it in the spring when brooks sing down from the highlands. Sometimes after a drenching rain in late fall when the ground is frozen, water may once again fill the pond. But the water pours through broken gaps in the old dam with its upended granite stones.

Old journals and diaries tell us that as soon as a group of families settled in a region, very soon there was a store, a blacksmith shop, and a gristmill. A miller often built his own mill. He built a dam to impound the water; he constructed an overshot or undershot wheel and fashioned the cog gears and wooden shafts. He fitted the stones for the grinding and kept them sharpened. Men and boys brought bags of wheat and corn to the mill on their shoulders; they came on horseback with the grain they had raised among charred stumps that marked the cemetery of virgin trees.

The gristmill was a pivotal center of the community. As their grain was being ground, men discussed the problems of citizenship in a new land and talked over the news that came in from seacoast towns. They gathered gossip to take back to their womenfolk on the lonely farms, and they debated the future that was burgeoning before their eyes.

As the men talked, the miller pulled the big wooden lever that freed the water from the mill pond and sent it over or under the wooden paddle wheel. The wheel started to groan and turn the wooden shafts and cogwheels that transmitted power to the grooved millstone. The upper rotating stone was supported on a drive shaft or spindle at just the precise height to pulverize the grain and produce

the grist that worked along the grooves to the outside. The lower, or nether, stone was called the bed stone. Grain was fed into the upper stone through the spout, called a "shoe." The grooves in the upper stone were cut by specially made picks. "Dressing a millstone" was the work of a craftsman, and in busy seasons a miller had to "dress" his stone frequently to keep a sharp grinding edge.

Today you see the old millstones used as decorative motifs in yards of summer homes, antique shops, and country inns. Trees surround the dams and ponds; the birches and alders, sumacs and tangled vines hide the channel where a wooden wheel turned and furnished power that helped a community become part of a nation.

When I was a boy, one of my favorite spots was the livery stable. When I walked into Woodward's Livery behind the Forest House Hotel, I was met by a pungent heady fragrance compounded of hay, leather, grain, harnesses, stained and splintered floor planks, and manure.

On brittle zeroish days, or when a honed-edge wind was swirling snow over fields, meadows, and upland mowings, I hitched Old Jerry to the pung, and my three sisters and I drove the mile and a quarter from Glenrose Farm to the village. We put a lighted lantern under the buffalo robe to keep warm. We didn't think of staying home from school just because it was cold. I dropped the girls at the village school on the common and then put up Old Jerry in the livery stable. At noon hour, the other boys and I walked over and fed the horses. Then at four o'clock, we hitched up and headed for home. In those days school began at nine o'clock and ended at four—that is, if you didn't have to stay late.

The time I most enjoyed the livery stable was on a Saturday when Father said, "Better get us a couple bags of middlings, a couple ground oats, and a bag of cottonseed meal." If you took out the rear seat of the pung, you could easily stack in several bags of grain. On a winter Saturday when work wasn't pressing, a forum gathered at the livery stable and a lad learned a good deal if he kept his ears open. The livery man was a horse trader, and so were most of the farmers and villagers. A farmer needed heavy horses for working, but good farmers and the leading men of the village were also interested in a good roader.

It was usually a comfortable 80 degrees in the livery office, and the fragrance of felt leggings, rubber arctics, sheep-lined coats, and the sawdust box for tobacco juice blended very pleasantly with the over-all aroma of the establishment. A lad listened to the men talk of weather and roads, cattle and horses. He heard tall tales told with sober faces and learned that truth and a sober mien are often strangers. Perhaps he picked up a little interesting gossip to take home to Mother, who had probably heard it already on the party line. And as he stood around the edges of the group, he thought of the day he would be big enough to join the men in the inner circle.

I liked the general store even better than the livery stable. Do you remember that pungent smell when you went into the general store? It was a peculiarly satisfying blend of coal oil, freshly ground coffee, strong cheese, plug tobacco, salt codfish, dried prunes, rubber boots, felt leggings, dill pickles, molasses, kegs of nails, crackers in an open barrel, gingham cloth, and harness leather.

NEW ENGLAND FLAVOR

Fogg's General Store—Grain, Coal, Groceries, Notions, Tobacco, and Candy. It was an important institution, circa 1910. A lad hitched his chunky sleek Morgan mare to the cedar rail in front of the porch and tossed a handsome plaid blanket over her while he went in to do an errand. You could buy anything from a mowing machine to a bottle of the Wine of Life—that wonderful tonic that warmed your interior and cured practically every affliction, and was "especially efficient in dissipating that tired feeling."

In the rear center of the store, a tall, cast-iron, potbellied stove shed radiant warmth. It sat on a zinc mat which was covered with an inch of stained sawdust. Plug tobacco was considered an essential by certain citizens, and storekeepers knew from experience that not all men were accurate when it came to aiming at an open stove door. Farmers and villagers gathered around the stove in the late afternoon to wait while the mail was being sorted in the corner post office.

Along the middle of the store, a wide counter was heaped with clothing: heavy union suits, men's woolen pants, colorful mackinaws, woolen shirts, white shirts, high rubber boots, leather boots, and felt leggings. There were eye-arresting horse blankets and cotton-flannel blankets; on a swinging shelf above were hats and caps, mittens and gloves.

The grocery counter was to the right with its wheel of cheese, coffee grinder, and box of salt codfish. On the shelves behind the counter were the common household items: tea that came in a big box with strange signs, patent medicines for both man and beast, open wooden firkins of chocolates and penny candies. By the side of the counter was an open barrel of common crackers into which men felt free

58

to dip. But you had a pretty good idea that the storekeeper kept a sharp eye peeled, and if you overreached the bounds of logical free-loading, you paid for it in later dealings.

Along the left side, as you entered the store, was the notions counter and behind it a wall lined with shelves. Here were the things that women studied on Saturday evenings when families came to do the weekly trading. After Mother had bartered her pound prints of butter with the four-leaf-clover design and had sold the eggs, she and my three sisters spent most of their time at this counter.

The hogshead of molasses with its wooden spout was at the rear, and most families bought the brown tangy liquid by the gallon. The molasses barrel was a big heavy affair, and when one arrived by freight train at the depot it was rolled from the freight car across a strong plank to the freight shed. Then it was rolled through the freight shed to an open door and down another plank to a solid two-horse wagon. At the store, it was rolled from the wagon to the back shed and onto its wooden cradle. The wooden spigot was driven in, and over the weeks that followed, the molasses was drawn out to farm and village families in one-gallon earthernware jugs.

Farmers spoke ahead for the empty hogshead. It was heavy and solid, and made a good watering trough when cut in two. It was also used with the head knocked out as a scalding tank at butchering time. And while I, of course, wouldn't know about such things, there were rumors that certain citizens filled the barrels with apple juice in the fall. Apparently they were not interested in fresh cider, for according to reports the barrels were left in the cellar all winter and not sampled until haying time.

But the boys were interested in the barrel for another reason. When the molasses was gone and the old store-keeper said they could roll the barrel out, it was a touchy proposition, especially if a number of lads had their eyes on it. The point was that if the barrel sat in the warm sun for a spell, the surplus liquid drained down to the bottom. Then the spigot was knocked out and a bunch of boys, myself included, went to work with long slender pieces of wood. We pushed them in the hole, scraped around for a while, and came out with a load of semisolid delicious molasses sugar.

There are two general approaches to a molasses barrel when you're interested in harvesting the sugar. You can be patient for a few days until the sun and heat have worked their magic and the gooey, flavorful, old-fashioned molasses has semicrystallized into a confection that reminds you of taffy. But this approach had an element of danger. If a sizable number of boys knew about the empty barrel, there was always the possibility that the sugar would be gone before you got there. The other approach was the immediate one. As soon as a barrel was rolled out back and placed in warm sunshine, you got to work and had your fill.

I never went into Fogg's General Store without wondering how soon that molasses barrel would be empty. But pretty soon my attention wandered to the penny candy and all the other things I wished I was rich enough to buy. Fogg's was more than a place of business, however. It was a focal point for part of the town's social and civic life. Around that old stove, men discussed local, state, and national politics. While they waited around for their womenfolk to make up their minds what they were going to buy, the men often cooked up a smart trade.

"Heard you was thinking of selling your old mare, Jim."

"No, I wasn't thinking of selling. Just happened to mention the other day at mail time that I didn't need three horses. Besides, Bessie isn't old, Amos. She's a mighty dependable mare. Can't be over eight or ten, maybe eleven."

"I'm not really thinking of buying, Jim. Just heard you wanted to sell. Did you hear about the new school teacher and how she went riding with that slick city drummer the other night? Heard she didn't get home until way after ten o'clock. Kinder risky, don't you think?"

"Could be. Though I don't think the drummers today are what they used to be. Now you take back about 1890, those drummer fellows were real actors. The last twenty years things have been going downhill. Look at these newfangled smelly contraptions they call automobiles. Go twenty miles an hour, I hear. Human beings weren't meant to go through life that fast. You thinking of getting another horse, Amos?"

"No, just heard you wanted to sell Bessie, Jim."

"Don't really want to sell. Bessie's a good-looking mare. Dependable too. 'Course if you needed another horse and the price was right I might trade. But I'd hate to see Bessie go. Got her last year from Bill Adams over in Hilltown. Bill said she was dependable. And she is. Say, Amos, has the road agent fixed up that mud hole over on your road? Heard tell you was a little stirred up over it."

"No, that dad-lazy rascal's been fixing up all the roads around town except mine. Over two weeks I couldn't get to town last April. We raised twelve hundred dollars at town meeting for roads and Seth's been spending money everywhere except over our way. I'm a taxpayer and I'm entitled to a good road like everyone else. How old did you say Bessie was?"

"She's probably going on ten or eleven, Amos. Might be twelve, but it's kinder hard to tell. Teeth are good and she's fat as a butterball. Good mare, Bessie, and dependable. Hate to see her go. She's a regular member of the family. Every morning she whinnies when I open the barn door, and she'll nuzzle me until I give her a lump of sugar or a piece of cookie. Has a sweet tooth, Bessie does. You need another horse?"

"No, don't really need one. But I sold one of mine last week and I like to keep three horses. When work is rushing it's good to have a spare. Heard you was over to Centerville to see your wife's folks last Sunday. They all well?"

"Yes, pretty good. Her folks are getting along but they keep tolerable. Her father's rheumatism kicks up in stormy weather. What sort of a horse you looking for, Amos?"

"Wasn't really looking, Jim. Just inquiring round. You put a price on Bessie yet?"

"No. I like Bessie. Don't know whether I ought to sell her or not. Harvest season coming on and a man needs a spare horse, like you say. Bessie's dependable. Hate to see her go."

"What price did you say, Jim?"

"Well, if you're anxious to buy, Jim, I'd let her go for $75.00."

"Guess you don't care much whether you sell or not, Jim."

"Might shade it a little. But Bessie's worth $60.00."

"Don't think I'd want to pay over $45.00 for just a spare horse."

"Bessie's more than a $45.00 horse, Amos. She's dependable. How's the corn and oats this season?"

"Got a good crop, Jim. Never saw corn come along any better than it has this year. You want to consider $50.00 for Bessie?"

"Well, I might. I don't need a third horse right now, and besides I'm thinking of trading with Alvin Stevens. Says he might swap his young gelding for a couple of my Jersey heifers. Could you make it $55.00? Bessie's dependable, Amos."

"No. I don't think she's worth $55.00. But if you'll throw in a horse collar, a whiffletree, and a pitchfork, I'll give you $52.50 and I'll take her along home right now."

And that's how the trade went. Maybe two weeks later, Jim and Amos would see each other again at Fogg's.

"Afternoon, Jim."

"Afternoon, Amos."

"Thought you said Bessie was dependable. She balks every time she's asked to pull a load."

"That's what I said. She's dependable. She balks, Amos, if she's asked to work. You can depend on it every time. By the way, I heard Jethro Seldon over in Antrim is looking for a good dependable horse. You might drop around and see him. Crops growing well, Amos?"

While the men dickered around the store, the women gathered by the notions counter, talked over the upcoming Grange supper, and gave each other the news of their families. Some of it was good news, some of it was bad; and if a neighbor had some hard luck, quiet-voiced men agreed on who would do the chores and perhaps set a day when all would gather to put in the silage, saw up and put in the wood, or do other essential jobs. Neighborliness was the mark of a good citizen, and in Fogg's General Store, men and women made the decisions that were the flowering of neighborliness.

CHAPTER THREE

I T MAY be that a hard day's work makes a soft bed, and a man's memory can admittedly play tricks. But on Glenrose Farm when we had real winters and folks wore warm long ones, a feather bed was important. In zeroish weather, Mother heated soapstones, bricks, and chunks of smooth hard maple in the oven. These were wrapped in pieces of old flannel and placed in the beds half an hour before bedtime. Father and I had similar ideas. A man needed three warm spots, one for his shoulder, one for his hip, and one down where his feet would be.

The four-poster bed was one of the most important pieces of furniture on New England farms—important enough so that it often headed the list of articles in a will. The feather mattress and the four-poster were completely home-made affairs. New Englanders were craftsmen with saw and adze, plane and knife. The bed frame, made of maple, ash, or oak, was corded with hemp that had been spun by hand and then washed, pulled, and twisted into a strong rope. My bed beneath the eaves of Glenrose Farm was laced lengthwise and crosswise with cord that was pulled taut. Over the rope foundation was what I think Mother called the underbed. This was made of heavy ticking and filled with clean oat straw or corn husks. The ticking was homemade of flax—grown, processed, and spun on the farm.

Over the underbed came the feather bed proper. Housewives were proud of their feather beds. Goose feathers, according to my grandmother, were by far the best filling, but half a century ago goose raising was on the way out, so hen feathers were used on most farms. Sometimes the feathers of wild turkeys and ducks were used in feather beds, and some bed ticks were filled with wild pigeons' feathers. Pigeons, literally by the millions, flew sky trails in certain areas and came to roost and feed in vast beech forests. The farmers just went out and caught them with a slip and noose.

Each spring housewives put the feather mattresses over outdoor clotheslines to air and sun. Occasionally a housewife decided to wash and dry the feathers, and there are men and women today who can remember stirring the feathers in tubs and buckets as they dried on a sunny windless day.

On cold winter nights I liked to see a feather bed waiting, fluffed high, with three soapstones warming strategic spots. Give a boy a first-class feather bed, a few cotton blankets, a couple of homemade quilts, and a flannel nightgown long enough to wrap around his toes, and he can really get some sleep.

The trouble with getting in a feather bed is sooner or later you have to get out. But when that time comes, the best thing to do is get out fast, scoop up your clothes and race downstairs to dress by the parlor heater. I did just that on many a zeroish morning, and standing in the parlor with my teeth chattering, the first thing I put on were my long ones. There was no nonsense about long underwear in those days; you wore it and you were glad of the warmth.

My grandfather wore his long ones until the day he died. Sometimes his daughter and granddaughters tried subtle methods to modernize him, sometimes they tried frontal assault; but in either case Gramp saw through their conniving. For a good church deacon, Gramp had a snort that sounded more like a cuss word than any snort I ever heard.

Gramp didn't hold with automobiles. "Frighten teams and smell up the countryside," he growled. He didn't like telephones. "Folks spend too much time listening to other people's business." He was opposed to electric lights. "The human eye was never meant to endure such glare," he claimed. But if you wanted to get Gramp really stirred up, the quickest way was to talk about long underwear. This was back in the days when people began to wear the same kind of underwear in cold weather that they did in the summer. When Gramp first discovered that his granddaughters, blossoming into teen-age women, were using summer-weight pinkies in the winter, he had a subject for a speech any time anyone would listen.

For years solid New Hampshire citizens had worn Blue Contoocooks, made in Contoocook, New Hampshire. After the Civil War, George D. Peaslee of Hillsboro got the idea that insulation of this kind was needed in the cold

New England climate. It was underwear of the shirt and drawer type and was protection both day and night. You put a flannel nightgown over your Contoocooks, added heavy woolen socks and a woolen nightcap, and you were all set for a warm night's sleep.

Then along came the union suit. I wish someone would discover who first got the idea. At the turn of the century, the mail-order catalog put it tersely: "The greatly increased demand for men's union suits is due to their merit as a practical garment. Nearly every man has suffered from time to time the annoying tendency, particularly in warm weather, of his undershirt to roll up his back and the inclination of the drawers to slip to an uncomfortable position. This is all overcome by the simple, common sense garment called the union or combination suit. Try our union suits. They fit like the skin."

Union suits came in various kinds, weights, and colors. There were heavy, wool-fleece-lined, worsted, brown merino, silk and worsted, open-shoulder and closed front models, red, natural gray, double-breasted, Glastonbury, Dr. Wright's Blue Australia, camel's-hair, the ribbed type, and the extra heavy Alaska that was "made for the coldest climate."

Women wore them too. One featured model was the Ladies' Drop Seat Cotton Union Suit. The description was succinct. "Ladies' very heavy Egyptian Cotton Union Suit, ecru color, with soft fleece lining. Made with drop seat, same as children's. Buttons down the front. It will be observed that the seat buttons below the line of the corset. In this manner, a practical and comfortable drop seat is made, and is preferred to the other styles by many. Never before have we been so thoroughly satisfied as we are now with our stock of underwear. We will leave it to you if they are not beyond competition."

There were summer-weight union suits for both men and women. The ladies could also get Black Cotton Ribbed Tights of fine Egyptian cotton that reached from the waist to the ankle. If cotton was not acceptable, long tights came in half wool or all worsted. The catalog also offered a few very daring models of summer underwear that reached only to the knee.

The children's underwear department "was complete with the best varieties made at prices that admit of no competition." In the boy's section there was a good paragraph: "Union suits are in great demand today as they are a practical solution of many vexatious difficulties found in trying to keep drawers in their proper place on young boys."

As soon as my drawers were in their proper place and I had warmed myself up a little by the parlor stove, I high-tailed it for the kitchen. I was supposed to build a fire in the kitchen stove before I picked up my milk pail and lantern and headed for the barn. "Making a fire these cold mornings is a very necessary task," said the *New England Farmer* for January 1857. "And to do it certainly and quickly will save growls and whines. Not only will it prove a saving of passion, but also a saving of material. How perfectly it would wake up a lazy sleeping child if compelled to bounce out of bed at daylight of a winter's morning and light the kitchen fire. It sends the lazy sleeping blood to the remotest extremities and quickens the whole body. It vitalizes the whole man."

There is no doubt in my mind that lighting the fire in a dark clammy kitchen sent my "lazy sleeping blood" to my remotest extremities. At 6:00 A.M. on a winter morning it is just plain cold. That is why I was very particular about the kindling's being in place before I went to bed. I liked short pine branches jackstrawed over a few wads of crumpled newspaper; then I wanted a half dozen finely split pieces of gray birch. On top of this I placed two or three split pieces of oak, maple, or ash. Once I got the fire started, I hustled into my mackinaw, put on my cap with fur-lined ear protectors, pulled on felt leggings and arctics, and went out to the barn. Even in the winter we milked six or eight cows that had freshened in the fall. In half an hour the kitchen would be warm and Mother would start breakfast and put up the lunches for me and my three sisters to take to school.

One way to teach a person the importance of kindling is to put him in a cold kitchen. There are differences of opinion, of course, as to the best material for kindling. I have heard some men argue that finely split, completely dried hardwoods, such as rock maple, beech, or ash, were better than anything else because once they are ignited they burn longer and you are more certain the large, heat-giving pieces of wood will take hold. There are a few casual fire-builders who merely scoop up a dustpan full of debris from the woodshed floor. On Cape Cod, gathering baskets of pine needles for kindling is an old-time custom; perhaps it originated before the days of great abundance of paper. In some sections a big hogshead of "diddle-dees," the name given to the brown evergreen needles, was always kept well filled in the woodshed.

My favorite kindling was, and is, the small-diameter dead branches of white or red pines. When the evergreens grow thickly, the lower branches die. The wood is resinous and catches fire quickly. Cut into 18-inch lengths, pine limbs are the most efficient kindling I know. Gray or white birch, well dried and finely split, is also excellent kindling, but the resin in the pine seems to generate an intense heat that quickly ignites the main logs.

Today most boys do not have enough home chores to keep them busy and teach them patience. Suburban, town, and village homes no longer have a cow, horse, pig, and chickens. A lad may have to mow the lawn, but he usually has a power mower; if he doesn't, chances are the lawn is about the size of the guest towels that color-conscious hostesses drape around their bathrooms.

I had plenty of chores when I was a boy, and one of them was thawing out the barnyard pump. Father and I had an efficient morning work routine. I dressed and started the kitchen fire while Father went to the barn. We needed running water in the milk house and barnyard trough, and I knew if the temperature had dropped around zero or below, the barnyard pump was sure to be frozen solid. So after I got the kitchen fire going in good shape, I set the two big copper teakettles full of water over the front cover. While I helped Father milk the cows, the kettles came to a boil. Most of the time the two kettles held just the right amount of boiling water.

Thawing out a pump teaches a boy patience, judgment, and care. You can't hurry a cold pump. By experience you learn that if you pour the hot water down too fast, not

71

only do you gain nothing in time so far as thawing out is concerned, you also run out of hot water and that means starting all over again.

I started with the first teakettle and poured in just a little water and began to work the handle up and down. There was a loose, coughing gurgle; the metal made high-pitched squeaking noises. Slowly I continued to pour in the water, and the steam from it made a thick vapor in the air. As I pumped the handle up and down slowly, the easy, meaningless gurgle continued. I kept pouring and pumping. When I finished one teakettle I snatched up the other. Still that hollow-sounding noise.

I didn't begin to worry until the second kettle was about half gone. That was when will power was required. I was tempted to pour in the rest of the hot water all at once. I knew I shouldn't, because I had tried it before without any luck. And if I succumbed to temptation, it meant going into the house, putting on two more kettles, and waiting. If there was anything in this world that required true patience, it was waiting for two kettles to come to a boil on a zero morning while you stood around.

So I kept pumping; I kept pouring that trickle of hot water down the pump's throat—teakettle in one hand, pump handle in the other. Then just as I was really beginning to wonder, I heard a slight change in the music. That indefinite, slurping, hollow, meaningless noise deepened to a basslike gurgle. In a few seconds I felt the pump catch for the first time.

Unless you've thawed out a pump, you can't imagine the feeling of relief that comes when you hear that gurgle. It was the same feeling I got when I was churning and it seemed as though the butter would never come. When the cream began to coagulate it made a different sound and I knew my task was nearly over.

The pump gurgled a few more times as I poured in the last drop of hot water. Suddenly my patience was rewarded; the water began to gush out. I carried some water to the milk house, and Father said, "Pump working, Haydn?"

"Yes, sir." I said.

"Well then," Father said, "let's go get some breakfast."

Wood was a vital commodity on Glenrose Farm. So far as fuel for the big kitchen stove and the nickel-trimmed parlor heater was concerned, there were five distinct phases: chopping, getting it up, sawing, splitting, and finally, wheelbarrowing it into the woodshed. It took a sizable amount of wood to provide heat in both stoves from fall until late spring, and of course there had to be wood for summer cooking and baking. I always enjoyed working with wood, and it's probably a good thing, because taking care of the wood supply was one of my most important chores.

It was fun to go to the wood lot with Father on a Saturday and cut wood for next season's fuel. I cannot say that pulling a crosscut saw was any particular pleasure, although it always gave Father a chance to get off his standard joke to the effect that he didn't mind pulling me, but he wished I wouldn't drag my feet. What I enjoyed most was using the axe. I enjoyed limbing out the trees that we felled for timber; but it was more fun when Father designated smaller maples and oaks that should be cut to give room for the better trees to develop. Scientific forestry had not yet come into its own, but Father treated our woodland acres as a renewable crop. Before we cut white pine, Norway pine, hemlock, or larger hardwood trees to be worked into boards and dimension stuff, he studied the situation and we cut trees that were "ripe." Where the maples were growing too thickly, we cut out enough to let the others grow more rapidly; and there were stands of oaks that needed thinning.

Each of us had his favorite axe. A good farmer is as choosy about his axe as he is about his hoe. Probably my first axe was the three and a half-pound Niagara Boys' Handled Axe that had a 28-inch handle. Today, when I go into a wood lot to chop, I still like a lightweight axe.

74

Father liked a medium-weight, double-bitted axe about five pounds in weight.

Probably the first tool that primitive man fashioned was a crude hammer; but it is possible that the second was an axe, made of stone chipped along one end for a full cutting edge. In terms of the thousands of years that man has been designing tools and gadgets to make life more comfortable, and more complicated, the history of the modern axe is but a momentary flicker of time. Each passing year the axe, as a tool, becomes less important, but when I was a boy, an axe was a cherished tool—as important as it was two centuries and more ago when a pioneer with rifle, axe, and hoe headed out from the safety of settled communities along the eastern coast and trekked west to hew a home and farm from the wilderness. Half a century ago, if a man needed a new axe, he had his choice among many styles and weights. For when it comes to choosing a new axe, a man is very particular. There's a certain feel, a "hang" to it, that tells you whether it fits your individual needs. It is a combination of vital factors: weight and shape of the head, the size and length of the handle, the way it seems to respond to muscular energy.

Special axes were made for particular purposes. There were the broad adzes, with a bite up to seven and a half inches in width, used for hewing large timber that framed barns and houses, for solid sills placed on granite-walled cellars, and for covered-bridge timbers. There were narrower carpenters' adzes for use on small timbers. Early in the history of axe making, men made double-bitted axes, for they discovered that two blades, each made for a separate purpose, helped a woodsman. A thin cheek just back

75

of the cutter edge is good for straight-grained hardwoods, but you need a thicker cheek for certain softwoods and for cutting off limbs.

An old catalog description puts it well. "Our best axe. Patented, easy chopping, hollow ground. A new innovation that promises to be the axe of the future for the reason that it is the easiest chopping axe in the world. The axe is hollow ground. It enters and leaves the wood with the least possible amount of resistance, and considerably less grinding is necessary to keep it in good condition. Not only the best and easiest chopping, but the handiest axe on the market today. Weighs from 3 to 5 pounds. Warranted. Price 63 cents."

Father taught me the four basic rules about chopping wood: make the cut on the opposite side to which you want the tree to fall, take advantage of every possible lean of the tree, make a good-sized notch, and keep your eye on the butt when the tree begins to fall.

My favorite wood for chopping was, and still is, the humble gray birch. I know that many good countrymen will scoff at the idea of gray birch in comparison with the hardwoods, but we discovered early on Glenrose Farm that if gray birch is handled correctly it makes good fuel. The secret is to get it cut, sawed, and stored under cover in just as short a time as possible. True, it is a quick-burning fuel in comparison with dry oak, maple, or ash, but the other side of the matter is that it throws a hot heat. Mother always wanted gray birch for use in the summertime, and called it "supper wood" because it gave a quick satisfactory fire to make supper biscuits and heat up the fried potatoes.

One of my easiest chores was gathering up winter kindling. It was enjoyable and light work. In the pine grove above the orchard, the white and red pines had many dead branches. As evergreen trees reach upward to the light in crowded areas, the lower limbs die. It was these dry, hard, resin-filled limbs that we favored for winter kindling. We could knock off some of the limbs with axes, and we had small curved saws fastened to six- and eight-foot handles that allowed us to saw off branches to a considerable height. We took branches as little as a half inch and as big as our wrists. We cleared the limbs of small side shoots and loaded the wagon high. Once we got the branches of varying lengths into the woodshed and under cover, the limbs could be cut later into fifteen-inch lengths on rainy or snowy days. The important thing with kindling, as with shocked corn and stacked beans, was to get it under cover when it was bone dry.

There was more to getting the winter's kindling than just the labor of another farm job. There is something about December that appeals to those whose hearts are tuned to the changing seasons. You know that time is sliding steadily downhill to the solstice; you know the time of dormancy has started. Perhaps that was why it was so pleasant to work among the pines in December. The carpet of needles was soft and springy; beneath my feet the magic process of humus making was going on—the process that means the release of elements for the continuance of life. The air was bracing and fragrant; the trees, looking like green ladies, talked and murmured as the wind moved their branches. In the pleasant peacefulness of the evergreens, with chickadees chanting an altoish song, and the

77

riveting of a distant woodpecker echoing from the maple sugar bush, I harvested a rich crop of memories.

Toward the end of winter, another one of my favorite chores was "getting up" the wood. That was a term we always used for hauling the wood from the wood lot to the yard behind the house and stacking it, ready for the saw rig. It was always more fun to do a job that involved the Morgan mare. Belle was sleek, plump, and friendly; she was high-lifed and a fast stepper. In the winter when there wasn't too much farm work, she was especially full of ginger and liked to break into a trot.

On a sunny Saturday when you could see spring in the year's eyes and the blue sky was patched with cumulus clouds, I hitched the mare to the big bobsled, and drove across the upland pasture and into the wood lot where the chopped wood was stacked in piles. I threw the handsomely colored blanket over the mare and loaded on the wood. Sometimes it was in four-foot split pieces, trunks of larger hardwoods that had been split with wedges and sledge hammers. Sometimes there were piles of long saplings we had thinned from a stand of young maples, oaks, or beeches. If we had cut hemlock and pine logs for shingles, boards, and dimension stuff, we trimmed out the larger limbs for house fuel and loaded the logs on the sled. I felt no particular pressure as I worked along. I could take my time and do a bit of exploring in the evergreens to see if the rabbits had been out the night before. I could even hunt around for a little spruce gum if my winter's supply was getting a bit low.

I never felt quite as happy about twitching out. That was hard work. Toward winter's end we would have quite a few logs in the wood lot between our orchard and Hayward's. It was my job with Old Jerry to twitch out the logs to a bank at the wood's edge, where the logs were piled ready for loading on the two-horse bobsled. If there had been snow storms since the logs were cut, you could tell their location by the smooth white lengths that made me think of pieces of chimney piping. I knocked away the snow at one end, used the peavey or a smooth piece of oak sapling to get room enough for the chain, hitched on Old Jerry, and twitched the log out to the loading pile.

It sounds simple and uncomplicated, but sometimes it involved a little more work. If there had been sleet and rain followed by a zero spell, an eight- or ten-foot log could be an obstreperous thing. If I couldn't get the chain under the end by making a hole with peavey or sapling, then I used an old dull axe to cut away the needles, leaves, and frozen humus. Occasionally I had to use a chain with a big hook and let Old Jerry pull at right angles to get the log loosened.

Old Jerry and I worked together well. Once the log pile was started, he knew the job as well as I. I fastened the reins on the hames and worked him by voice. He geed and hawed instantly at command. He would pull the log in beside the pile, wait while I used the peavey to roll the log against the others, then he would follow at my heels back into the woods for the next log.

Sawing, splitting, and getting the wood into the woodshed wasn't very much fun either—and I didn't have Old Jerry to help me. Sawing was just a routine job. Each spring Leslie Carr came with his saw rig, drawn by two white horses, and pulled up right beside the wood stacked in

79

the yard. A steam engine provided power for the saw, and I can still hear that chugging engine and remember how the chugs grew farther apart and weaker in volume as the saw bit through a large oak or maple log. Mr. Carr pushed the wood against the whirling teeth that screamed when they bit into hardwood knots. Father took the sawed-off pieces and tossed them away. It was my task to lift the pieces onto the saw table—and most of the time I had to hustle.

Splitting straight-grained chunks wasn't too bad, but the less said about the job of wheeling wood into the woodshed the better. That was a monotonous job in my book. I had to wheel most of the split wood into the shed and stack it into high tiers. This was the wood for the kitchen stove. For baking, Mother liked the long-burning steady heat that split maple and oak gave. And a couple of pieces of sugar maple or white oak kept the fire going in the forenoon and afternoon stretches. The gray birch, her "supper wood," went under cover quickly and by summer it was dry enough to burn well.

I had to put the tough knotty chunks of wood into a special pile. They were so irregular in size that I couldn't stack them in tiers. We usually had quite a pile, because there is nothing to equal a knotty chunk of hardwood for the parlor heater along about nine in the evening when it is bedtime. If the drafts are carefully regulated, it means a bed of coals in the morning, so that the fire can be started up quickly.

I can still see that woodshed with its high tiers of split wood. "Keep the outside edge just a little higher," Father always said, "and the tiers won't tip over." And I can see that symphony of colors in tans and browns, pale yellows and grays. I can smell that heady satisfying fragrance from the hardwood and hemlock, the birch and the apple.

Home remedies and medicines were standard equipment on Glenrose Farm. Mustard-plaster and onion-syrup time began in the late fall and continued through the winter, and we knew that come April, Mother would start to dose us up with sulfur and molasses; and neither Father nor I could devise any technique for thwarting her determination.

I wish I could remember exactly how Mother made that mustard plaster. It always followed a definite procedure. I would come in from school or chores and unthinkingly give a little hollow cough. Mother's eyes would sparkle and her jaws would set. "You're catching a cold, Haydn. I'll fix you a mustard plaster, and you take a spoonful of onion syrup before and after meals for a while."

Then she got busy and mixed up the mustard with lard. The resulting mess was spread on a square of heavy cloth material, perhaps a foot each way; then this square was fixed with safety pins to my union suit. Mother made a fresh plaster each day. Naturally a lad did not take off his union suit at night—not in a New Hampshire winter in an unheated upstairs bedroom. Therefore, I got the benefit of the mustard plaster on a 24-hour basis until Mother decided the cold or cough was over.

I didn't object too much to either the plaster or the onion syrup. The syrup soothed my throat and slid down very amiably. The grated onion was mixed with plenty of sugar and possibly some other flavoring. The result was

81

a thick, tangy-sweet liquid that did the job it was supposed to do.

One home remedy that I never heard of in another family was Father's technique for drying up a cold or a dripping nose. We called it the "hemlock cigar." He or I would get a quart or so of hemlock needles and put them in a pan in the oven for an hour or more until the moisture was practically dried out. We made the wrapping by taking a piece of paper about six inches square and rolling it up, cornerwise, on a lead pencil. Then we filled the "cigar" with the dried hemlock needles and had a smoke that we believed dried up nasal passages.

I haven't had a drink of thoroughwort tea since I was a boy, but if memory serves correctly, thoroughwort or boneset, as it was often called, was not too bad. Like sulphur and molasses, it was supposed to thin out your blood, and nobody ever thought about going into the spring without doing that.

My Grandmother Pearson had very definite ideas about spring tonics. She knew they were necessary, and she knew that her tonics were the best. When Father bought Glenrose Farm, Grandmother came to visit us each spring thereafter as long as she could. She came down from the old Pearson mountainside farm in Madison, New Hampshire and brought an arsenal of spring medicines with her. Sulphur and molasses was too easy for Grandmother; she went well beyond that. She had personally evolved various tonics and bitters, and for more than half a century she had tried them on her family, relatives, and friends.

Grandmother was a lady of the old school, with determination and zeal, and brooked no nonsense when April's tonic time arrived. "You are looking peaked, Frank," she would say to Father. "We'll start on the tonics in the morning."

"Mother," Father said in self-defense, "Haydn and I have decided to use just rhubarb and dandelion greens this year. Both are excellent tonics."

"Nonsense," Grandmother answered. "Just because you have a college education and know a lot of words I don't, is no sign you know how to take care of yourself. Both you and Haydn are looking peaked; your blood needs thinning and we will start in the morning."

Father knew from years of experience that he was on the losing end, and I also quickly learned to accept the inevitable. Grandmother timed her visits to dose us up and we had to take her medicine. I enjoyed hearing Father talk back to his mother, and I can still see her twinkling eyes as he pleaded the goodness of rhubarb and the benefits of dandelion greens boiled with salt pork. He would put on an eloquent act describing the help the human system received from young shoots of pokeweed and from stems of lamb quarters. He would orate fervently over the deliciousness of fiddlehead greens. Grandmother, with a tight-lipped smile and crinkled eyes, enjoyed her son's act; perhaps she was seeing Father as a small boy again in the kitchen in the farm on the mountainside. But Grandmother always said, "We'll start in the morning."

As I recall, she gave me and my three sisters sulphur and molasses each afternoon when we returned from school for about ten days; each morning before breakfast we had a spoonful of one of her precious tonics that she concocted from barks, plant stems, plant roots, and blossoms. And

while we were thinning our blood streams, we wore an asafetida bag beneath our long underwear. Unless you are personally acquainted with the aroma of this fetid Oriental gum, you cannot comprehend the meaning of spring a few decades ago. Day and night we wore that bag; the smell in the hot school room was something to lift the scalp. Mrs. Meigs, our beloved teacher, said more than once that the only thing she disliked about teaching was asafetida time.

Grandmother's tonics were not too bad; they were sharp, tangy, and full-bodied. From her cherished recipes she compounded brews that took the essence of yellow dock, dandelions, wild cherry bark, mandrake, and many other plants. The simmering process was long; she strained the liquid and used a piece of hard rock candy in each bottle before they were put away on a shelf in the earth-floored cellar of the farm home. There were rumors that certain citizens used to take some of their wives' bottles of tonics and mix the liquid with hard cider, but I wouldn't know about such goings-on.

MEMORIES OF A COUNTRY BOYHOOD

I do know a little about some of the tonics available from the mail-order catalog. There were such liquids as Wine of Life, the Marvellous System Builder, Orange Stomach Bracer, and the Peruvian Wine of Cocoa, to name just a few. Deacon Ward, who used to begin our Sunday school class by passing around a bag of horehound drops, put his faith in Compound Extract of Sarsaparilla. He used to say to me, "There's no use taking chances with New Hampshire spring weather. You never know what you have developed during the winter. And just look at what this Compound Extract will do for you."

You couldn't doubt it, for it was right there in black and white for all to read: "For scrofula, sarsaparilla is the greatest known remedy, and there is no other disease that is so general among our population. Almost every individual has this latent disease coursing in his veins. Its alarming fatality is not realized because consumption and other diseases are reported as the cause of deaths, many of which are the result of scrofula. The symptoms of scrofula are many and varied: pallid countenance, a bluish-white transparent complexion, inflamed eyelids, eruptions on the scalp and various parts of the body, irregular appetite, bowels irregular, a general lassitude and debility which takes away all energy and a desire for action, business or labor.

"Scrofula is most dangerous when it seats itself upon the lungs. It is not, however, confined to any part of the body as it attacks the liver and kidneys, also the digestive and uterine apparatus, inducing and often resulting in a long train of diseases such as consumption, ulceration of the stomach, tumors, erysepellis, salt rheum, blotches, pistales, scald head, catarrh, dyspepsia, female weakness, dropsy, emaciation, general debility and that tired feeling."

If there were that many things hanging over your head, wasn't it a matter of simple common sense to buy some Compound Extract of Sarsaparilla and ward off the dangers? I agreed with the Deacon; prudence dictated the answer and there was no logical alternative. The fact that the good Deacon took care that Mrs. Ward didn't know about the sarsaparilla has no bearing on the subject. The Deacon was sensible and he was generous. He always gave me a small amount while he had a full cupful. He kept the bottles hidden under the debris beneath the workbench in his cluttered farm shop. On cold blustery April days there was something about that Sarsaparilla Compound that warmed your innards and gave you a sense of security that you were fending off a multitude of dangers.

We had a wide choice of tonics, cures, bitters, extracts, and body builders if we decided we needed a little medication. One pleasant-tasting spring drink was Peruvian Wine of Cocoa, "well known throughout Europe for its nourishing and strengthening qualities. It nurtures and refreshes both the body and the brain and has deservedly gained its excellent reputation and superiority over all other tonics. It is especially adapted for persons in delicate health and convalescents. It is very palatable and agreeable to take and can be borne by the most enfeebled stomach when everything else would fail. It is used in most of the hospitals in Europe, and many of our American public institutions are adopting it. After many severe tests it has been effectually proven that in the same space of time more than double the amount of hardship and work could have been undergone when Peruvian Wine of Cocoa was used and positively no fatigue experienced."

The celery-malt compounds were supposed to be excellent, but they had a bitter, mouth-puckering taste that acted as a deterrent to consumption. The Orange Wine was a trifle more pleasant, but it too was bitter. One good spring tonic that contained the spirit of the new season was Wine of Life, or Vin Vitae. It added authority, somehow, to have the Latin words used in big type. This was advertised in a hard-hitting way by a series of logical questions: Are you easily tired? Do you sleep badly? Are you nervous? Do you feel exhausted? Have you lost your appetite? Is your stomach weak? Are you thin? Is your circulation poor?

Chances are at least one of the questions would hit home, and you were convinced that a dram or two of Wine of Life would do the trick. "Vin Vitae," the description read, "is a preparation combining through highest medicinal skill the curative, healing, and strengthening powers of celebrated vegetable elements, procured from medicinal South American herbs, with the invigorating tonic effect of the prest and finest wines of sunny California. The herbs supply the needed food strength for the blood and nerves, the wine counteracts the disagreeable, nauseous property of the herbs and gives just the right fire and life to the preparation.

"Vin Vitae makes women strong. Weak women, easily tired, worn out by ordinary household duties, should take Wine of Life regularly as a tonic. Vin Vitae is giving thousands of women health, beauty and freedom from the dragging pains which have made their lives so miserable.

Vin Vitae corrects all ailments peculiar to the sex, regulating the system, stops the pains, tones up the nervous organisms, brightens the eye, clears out the complexion, rounds out the figure, and retains health."

As I look back, I realize that citizens who strenuously objected to sulphur and molasses had no objection whatever to many of the commercial bitters and tonics. Since Father was a minister and Mother's nose was peculiarly keen, I had to use judgment, of course, when I went to Deacon Ward's to see how things were with him. But even as a teen-ager I needed a tonic just as much as he did. I always had some of the symptoms listed in the catalog description, and with the farm's hard spring work coming on, it was my duty to get myself in as good physical shape as possible.

My favorite of all mail-order tonics was Blackberry Balsam Compound, for it cost only 20 cents for a big bottle. Deacon Ward was very fond of it too. Sam Adams, the bachelor farmer across the road from the Deacon, ordered the latter's supply, and on a Saturday when Mrs. Ward was attending an all-day meeting of the Missionary Society or quilting in the Ladies' Sewing Circle rooms, we men moved the liquid from Sam Adams's place to the Deacon's farm shop. The Blackberry Compound was sweet, smooth, and heavy enough so that it left a good lingering aftertaste. There was no question of its efficacy, for the catalog listed a goodly number of conditions that it would alleviate. "It is a household remedy in the fullest sense of the word," the description said. "It will be found helpful for infants, children and adults. The poorest in the land can afford it at 20 cents a bottle, and often it will be the means of saving life." Young and old alike could sip Blackberry Compound on a blustery April day and know they were doing the right thing.

When spring came to Glenrose Farm it brought a good deal more than sulfur and molasses and Grandmother's tonic. It brought a whole round of new chores—chores that would go on through the summer and into the fall.

One day about this time of year Father was likely to say, "Haydn, don't you think it would be a good idea to sprout the potatoes?" What Father meant was, "Haydn, sprout the potatoes before you do anything else." He believed in the indirect approach.

I can't say for sure how old I was when Father first appointed me the official potato sprouter, but that's what I was.

Potato sprouting was not a glamorous job, but it had to be done. In late winter and early spring, long white slender tendrils sprout from the potatoes' eyes. You have to rub off the tendrils so the potatoes will keep in better condition through the spring. We planned to have new potatoes along with green peas on the Fourth of July, but if the Green Mountain potatoes were to keep in usable condition, they had to be sprouted periodically from April into June.

It is almost half a century now since I first started potato sprouting, but I remember the process and scene as if it were yesterday. I sat on a box on the floor of the potato bin. The bin was really the open space in the chimney foundation—an arch which supported the fireplaces and chimney. It was dark, as well as damp, in the earth-floored house cellar, so I needed a kerosene lantern for light. I can recall the smell in the cellar—a heavy damp pungent smell compounded of moist soil, potatoes, apples, carrots, turnips, salt pork, cold crackling brine, and the old floor boards. Probably there were some rotten potatoes and possibly a decayed cabbage or two, and if there is any farm-cellar fragrance equal to the combination of decayed potatoes and decomposed cabbages, I have yet to smell it.

Sprouting potatoes was a time-consuming, monotonous task. Each potato had to be picked up and the sprouts rubbed off. Father planned to sell several bushels of potatoes in late spring; they brought a good price at Fogg's General Store, and Glenrose Green Mountains were well known to the villagers who asked for them. So in addition to the sprouting, it was also a sorting job. The good-sized spuds with the best appearance were put in a special pile for the store.

It was cold and damp in the cellar. When I first sat down and began to sprout and sort, I looked at all the bushels ahead of me. I shook my head sadly and wondered if I'd get through in time to take a trip along the brook before dinner. I usually did, but it was a long, boring job anyway. Every once in a while, I got up and went over to the apple barrels and selected a big, wrinkled-skinned Golden Russet. Beneath that wrinkled, blotched skin was juicy, tangy flesh, and a Russet or two helped as I worked along at the Green Mountains.

Now that I come to think about it, potatoes played a pretty large part in my life. I remember the names of some of the varieties and the pride we took in our potato crop. We grew Early Rose, Irish Cobbler, and Green Mountains, but some of the other names were even more imaginative: Aroostock Beauty, Beauty of Hebron, Black Chenango, Country Gentleman, Early Peachblow, Pat Murphy, Quick Lunch, Cambridge Russet, Snowflake, White Mercer, and Sir Walter Raleigh.

New Hampshire claims to be the first area in this country to grow white potatoes in 1719. But the evidence is to the contrary. In *The History of Garden Vegetables* by E. L. Sturtevant, published in 1890, it says, "Potatoes were grown in Virginia in 1609, and are also mentioned in 1648 and 1650." So far as my research goes, it seems likely that white potatoes, native to South America, were brought into the southern regions of this country by the Spaniards. A clergyman, Chauncey Goodrich, is credited by some authorities with making the potato crop the inexpensive nutritious food that it has become. In the 1840's a devastating blight hit the crop in this country, and for several years the harvest was almost nil. Goodrich, knowing potatoes originally came from South America, sent there for some seed. He planted them near his church in Utica, New York, and from that source strong-growing potatoes gradually spread over the country. He labeled his variety the "Rough Purple Chili," and today that strain of potatoes is the ancestor of some 200 varieties and substrains.

On Glenrose Farm we planted, hoed, and dug potatoes by hand. As a matter of fact, we picked off potato bugs by hand too—or rather I did. It is a handsome bug if you can be objective about it. But handsome is as handsome does, and the bugs had to be eliminated. Picking potato bugs wasn't too bad a task. I rather enjoyed it, especially if the potato patch was out of sight of the house and my overly

91

conscientious sisters, who felt a moral obligation to keep track of my working habits, couldn't see me. The equipment was simple and inexpensive—a small can about half full of coal oil. I worked along the row, looking for the beetles; when I saw one, I picked it from a leaf and dropped it into the can.

There were two angles to the job that appealed to me. First, I could work by myself, and I enjoyed that. When a fellow is his own boss, he can decide whether to work fast or slow. Sometimes I felt one way; sometimes the other. Second, if, as I say, the patch of potatoes was at the low end of the field out of sight of the house, I could take time, periodically, to do some other things. I knew where woodchuck holes were located, and they needed studying. Usually there were a couple of large hornets' nests on the gray birches across the wall in the pasture. It was fun to get as close as possible and watch the papermakers come and go. There was one large flat rock near the pasture wall that a big black snake used year after year as a sunning spot. Sometimes I would trace a warbler to its nest or could see a mother partridge and a brood of bright-eyed little chicks. And after I got all that out of the way, I could go back to the potato patch and pick a few more bugs.

Speaking of angles, the best part about hoeing potatoes was swimming. Now that may sound strange, but here is the way it used to work. I would be hoeing along on a hot summer day. The sun poured down; it was getting toward four o'clock. I had been at it since morning and I was pretty tired. Of course, I had been to the kitchen several times to see how Mother was coming along with the baking and to stoke up on needed nourishment. But I felt I was about at the end of my rope.

Perspiration ran down the crease in my back; small pebbles had worked into the tops of my shoes. My hands, as my candid sisters remarked when I came into the kitchen, were only slightly darker than usual. My back was aching and the muscles along the backs of my legs were beginning to creak. Then Father wandered across the yard and stood for a minute inspecting the battleground. He glanced up at the lowering sun. "You've done a pretty fair job," he said. "Why don't you call it a day, get your swim, and then bring home the cows?"

Miracles still happen in this world! It's amazing how quickly my strength revived. It was a beautiful day after all. I set my hoe against the gate, called to Shep, and started on a run for the swimming hole in the creek. I raced across the meadow mowing with the farm collie bounding and barking beside me. Behind the clump of alders it was the work of seconds to pull off my shoes, socks, overalls, and shirt. For one glorious anticipatory moment I stood on the bank above the pool. Then I lifted my arms and dived into the cool water.

There are clear-cut distinctions in this world, and boys from eight to eighteen know that one of them has to do with bathing. In the winter when it is cold, and a young man is insulated by long ones, it is a waste of time and effort to get wet all over even once a week. But come warm weather, it is simply common sense for a young man to take a bath two or three times a day—in a swimming pool. It was a wonderful sensation when you were hot and dirty to dive into the cool water, swim under water for a few yards, and then come to the surface snorting and blowing.

The meadow pool wasn't very large, perhaps thirty feet long and fifteen or twenty wide, but it was large enough for a good swim. At one end, where the water flowed over the rocks that made a fording place for the hay wagons, trout lay in the stream facing the current. Sometimes I saw a big water snake, holding its head high as it slithered downstream. There were bloodsuckers that attached themselves to arms and legs, but that was a minor matter. Sometimes a kingfisher sat in the willow that stretched its branches over one side of the pool, and calmly watched while Shep and I thrashed around in the water. Right then and there, hoeing potatoes didn't seem so bad after all.

Digging potatoes was a fall job. When I returned home from school, I dug spuds for an hour or more on pleasant days. The soil was dry and crumbly so that the earth fell away easily. And on a sunny Saturday I put in a full day. I used a potato digger, of course. It was a stubby heavy tool, and I well recall Father's admonition to strike in a few inches from the hill; otherwise the tines might go into a good potato.

It wasn't the worst job on the farm, but it could get monotonous on a white-cloud, mellow day when a lad would like to be out in the woods or climbing the upland pasture. It was, however, a pretty picture to see the big-smooth-skinned Irish Cobblers and Green Mountains lying in the sun. After the potatoes were dried a bit, I picked them into a half-bushel basket and then poured them into burlap bags. Old Jerry and I hauled the potatoes to the barn or a shed, where they waited for sorting.

MEMORIES OF A COUNTRY BOYHOOD

We had three grades. Topflight, handsome potatoes went into a special bin in the earthen-floored house cellar; later in the winter or early spring when the price was up, these were potatoes that went to customers in the village and to Fogg's General Store—after I sprouted them. The medium-sized ones were for family use. The small ones I cooked in a kettle in the back yard along with cornmeal and pumpkins for the pigs. I guess I didn't mind hoeing and digging potatoes so much, especially when Mother had roast pork and made up some milk gravy to go with the potatoes.

The old farm shop was a relaxing place on a rainy raw day. It was a sanctuary for a lad and his father in bad weather any time of year, but I always liked the farm shop best in the spring. Our shop was a large room in the old two-decker barn that in earlier days had served as a horse barn. The big box stove threw a comfortable heat, and once the shop was up to 75 degrees, the outside world's chilliness mattered little. Cold rain might pour down in torrents; the fields and hills might be a sodden, brown-gray monotone hue. Muddy rivulets might trickle down the orchard road, flow around the silo and the end of the barn, and then spread out across the big farmyard. But inside the shop it was warm, dry, and comfortable.

The old shop was not an example of meticulous housekeeping, but a boy who was puttering along making some birdhouses knew where everything was and was happy in the clutter. The floor was covered with sawdust, shavings, mud, and miscellaneous dirt. The windows on the south and east sides of the room were streaked and grimy; patches of dust-crusted cobwebs filled the corners. The walls were covered with a score and one things, hanging from spikes driven into the two-by-fours.

I can still see those old faded horse blankets, once bright and colorful. There were worn-out horse collars and other pieces of harness, coils of rope, lengths of chain, half-bushel baskets, basket hooks for use in picking apples, the barrel header, hand rakes, shovels, and an old dung fork that for some reason hung unused behind the stove for many years. The corners of the shop were heaped with miscellaneous tools: old axes, a sledge hammer, crowbars, spades, log-splitting wedges. The two-man crosscut saw hung from a wooden peg in one corner. There were half-used bags of fertilizer and a wooden cask of shingle nails.

On the south side in front of the windows was the long wide workbench with its old-fashioned wooden vise at one end. At the back of the bench, heaped high in front of the windows, was a pile of odds and ends accumulated over the years. Beneath the bench was a tangle of lumber, short lengths of boards, pieces of dimension stuff—all covered with a layer of shavings and sawdust. But somehow, when you wanted a piece of either softwood or hardwood, you could always find what you needed.

Along the east side, between the windows, were a series of shelves where we kept a dozen and one cans filled with nails, tacks, screws, washers, and bolts. There were cans filled with turpentine in which paintbrushes were stored. There were cans half filled with different-colored paints. Father was particular about keeping equipment painted, and it was a spring job, on a good day when the soil was too wet for us to haul dressing, to paint the farm wagon, hay rake, plows, harrow, and cultivator. We used the old favorite—the light blue that was often called Dump Cart Blue. The fragrance in the shop was almost as good as the aroma in Fogg's General Store. It was a nostril-tickling, satisfying combination of fertilizers, paints, old leather, sawdust, cobwebs, rusty iron, and the smell of the hot stovepipe.

Here in the farm shop we mended rakes and cultivators, worked on whiffletrees and ladder rungs. We did most of our whittling here too. I can see Father now, sitting in an old delapidated chair, carefully whittling out a rake tooth or smoothing out the rough spots on a basket hook. Father always liked to keep a supply of various woods on hand for whittling. I remember how he would bring home a few branches when we took our Sunday afternoon walks. He needed the slender branches of a young maple for a rake tooth. For the basket hooks, he collected branches that grew at a sharp angle from the main stem. As for me, I usually collected forked branches for slingshots.

There are two kinds of whittling and I don't recall to which I was first exposed. You can whittle for fun or you can whittle for a purpose. In pioneering times, men and boys, in the light from cabin fireplaces, whittled out many objects for farm and household use. I have read that in the first days of frontier settlements, plates and bowls, forks and spoons were whittled from wood. Basswood, or whitewood, soft and straight-grained, was a favorite material. Whittling for a purpose is good. But when I was a boy I indulged in the other kind—that is, whittling for the sake of whittling.

I had a good knife, a lot of good soft wood, and the

97

farm shop was a perfect place for whittling. On many a rainy afternoon I whittled out my idea of a horse, a bear, or a lion, if there was nothing else to do. And every once in a while, I would get up and look through the pile of old mail-order catalogs or hunting and fishing magazines stacked in a corner of the shop.

"Still raining, Haydn?" Father would ask.

I would go to the door of the shop and look out over the flooded farmyard where raindrops were dancing in the puddles. "Yes, sir," I would say, and then get back to my whittling.

It must have been a picturesque scene a century and more ago. At early dawn while night's dew was still on the grasses, groups of men gathered at the edges of green mountain meadows, in lush river valleys, and at the borders of salt marshes along the coast. In those days the cutting of grass was done by hand with scythes and snaths. Farmers and their boys and hired men exchanged work in the year's major farm operations. When it came time to start haying, they gathered at a farm. Each man brought his own snath and two or three razor-edged scythes; and each man knew the width of the swath he could mow. One after another they set out, each mower waiting until the one before him had started. If a dozen men were mowing and the average mowed strip was five feet, it meant that one trip across the meadow, marsh, or upland field took down a sixty-foot strip of grass.

If your imagination is keen, perhaps you can hear the swish of those sharp-bladed scythes as they sliced through the green grasses. Mowing with a scythe was an art. At periodic intervals the men rested briefly; they put the end of the snath on the ground, pulled a whetstone from an overalls pocket especially designed to hold the long narrow stone, and proceeded unhurriedly, methodically, and skillfully to touch up the edge of the scythe.

The whetstone is the natural partner of the scythe, but as any good farmer knows, the grindstone plays an even more important part in keeping the edge of a scythe ready for use. Turning the grindstone was one of my chores. Father was very particular about his scythe, and the mowing-machine blades. The weather-beaten old grindstone sat in the shade behind the milk house. An old tin can with a small hole was fastened above the stone, so that water dripped constantly on it. I sat on a box and turned the iron handle. Father stood up and bore down hard if the scythe edge or one of the mowing-machine blades had a nick in it.

Sometimes it was comparatively light work, just putting on a good edge. Other times, if the scythe or blade had nicks to be ground out, Father bore down hard, and a fellow had to use all his muscle to keep the big heavy stone going at a good speed. When Father leaned back, took up the scythe and unhurriedly tested the edge with his thumb, I had to make a quick decision whether to let the momentum of the grindstone run down, or whether it would be better to keep turning.

I have been trying for years to find out who invented the first grindstone and where they were manufactured in New England. They were evidently a standard tool in 1860. This is what the *New England Farmer* of July 1860 says: "An axe to grind! Not one of your political ones, of which

100

we hear so much just now, but a real cast steel chopping axe, that has stood in the woodshed and been used whenever any of the men folks or the women folks have had occasion to hack, hew or split, during the past winter. Just see how blunt and thick the 'edge' is. What a grinding it must have.

"If the single experience of young Ben Franklin, one cold morning in grinding an axe, has added to the vocabulary of politicians one of their most expressive phrases, who will venture to compute the number of sea voyages that have been planned by farmers' boys at the crank of some old grindstone, or of resolutions formed to be a merchant, mechanic, peddler, anything so that they shall not be obliged to grind dull axes on miserable grindstones.

"In looking over the premises of our agricultural friends, admiring improvements that have been made, and discovering those that are projected, we instinctively look for the grindstone. If we find an ancient, sad-looking affair with wooden gearing, and leaning, it may be, against the wall for support, we feel like saying that which the proprieties of the occasion will not warrant. But if the grindstone is properly housed, hung on well oiled roilers, and with a treadle, so that one man can sharpen a tool without raising his neighbors, or coaxing his wife to turn 'just one minute' we feel assured that all is right. Depend upon it, as goes the grindstone, so goes the farm."

When it comes to whetstones, we have more information—or legend—about the origin of this sharpening abrasive. Whetstones have been used since time immemor-

101

ial. In the 13th chapter of First Samuel, verses 20 and 21, we find, "But all the Israelites went down to the Philistines to sharpen every man his share and his coulter, and his axe and his mattock."

Not long ago a group excavating in Egypt found a basket of tools in which was an oilstone. The archaeologists figured the tools dated back to about 1450 B.C. So far as I can find, the first account of sharpening stones in America mentions a Thomas Merton who made whetstones in what is now Wollaston, Massachusetts, in the 1600's. About 1815, stone was quarried in Arkansas and made into whetstones.

According to legend, Isaac Pike, of Haverhill, New Hampshire, who founded the Pike Manufacturing Company, discovered some stone in 1823 that put a good edge on his axe. That was the beginning of the whetstone business in northern New Hampshire. In the 1844 report of the *Geology and Mineralogy of New Hampshire,* the writer says, "Scythe stones are usually made of fine soft mica slate, consisting of mica and granular quartz. It is broken into pieces . . . roughly hewn with a hatchet, and then ground on a grindstone sprinkled with siliceous sand. . . . Their sharpening surfaces are dependent on the renewed surface of the siliceous particles, the mica wearing away as they are used."

I don't pretend to be an expert with scythe and snath, but in my time I have mowed a good bit by hand. At one end of our thirty-acre meadow on Glenrose Farm we had a swale spot. It was too mucky an area for the heavy work horses, even in a dry season, and it wasn't a pleasant experience to have a horse hitched to a mowing machine founder in the mud. But this area was a tremendous producer of coarse grass that we used for litter in the hen house, and I especially remember that we used it in the pigs' house in late fall, perhaps into January. So this swampy area was mowed by hand. I raked it with a bull rake and carried big forkfuls to the edge of the swale to load onto the hayrack. After I mowed a swath across the wet section, I stood the snath on end and sharpened the scythe with the whetstone.

Today, as I trim out around the walls and other spots here on my farm, and the metallic, monotone notes ring out in the air, I think of the music of the whetstones long ago when a group of men finished a swath across a field and touched up the edges of their scythes. That was the alto part of the music—a balance to the soft whish of keen blades laying low the grasses to wilt in the summer sun.

Summer on Glenrose Farm meant no school, swimming in the creek, and going around barefoot; but it also meant more chores and more time to do them. Picking blueberries was one that I didn't mind too much. Blueberry day was an important event in the year. Primarily the day was for a utilitarian purpose, for Mother canned many quarts of the fruit for winter use; but it was also a chance for a pleasant family outing.

We organized carefully for the blueberry trip to Will Stearn's farm on the north side of town. Will had a sizable pasture area studded with highbush blueberries where in a good season you could reap a satisfying harvest in a short time. Will charged a few cents a quart and you picked your own. The day before the trip, Mother cooked enough food for a dozen people. I can recall blueberry expeditions when several families agreed to go on the same day and it made a picnic as well as a working day.

We got up early, perhaps four-thirty, did the chores, put the cows to pasture, ate breakfast, and were on the road in the two-seated democrat by six o'clock. By six-thirty we were picking, and eating, blueberries to our hearts' content. I liked to pick highbush blueberries. I won't claim I was the best picker in the family, or the fastest, but I certainly picked my share and plopped them into the two-quart lard pail that was fastened under my suspender button. When that was full, it was poured into an eight- or ten-quart pail, and as the forenoon wore on, the pails gradually filled with the blue nuggets.

At noon we had a picnic with roast chicken, cold ham, homemade bread, jellies, pickles, cakes, pies, and cookies. I can remember the cold homemade root beer that we brought in a big bucket filled with ice. I can remember that some years one of the families brought a big freezer full of ice cream.

By mid-afternoon, the pails were filled and we started jogging homeward behind Old Jerry. The pails of berries were tucked under the seats of the democrat. Probably we had a pickup supper. Then came the job of sorting the berries. I can see Mother and my three sisters sitting there in the kitchen, working by the soft golden glow of kerosene lamps, sorting over the berries and preparing for the canning bee the next day. And most likely one of my sisters would say, "Look at all these leaves and twigs. I'll bet these are berries that Haydn picked." They probably were. I guess I just got careless when I started thinking about all the blueberry jam and pies we were going to have.

Father was particular about the red kidneys that we raised. Not that we had anything against yellow eyes or pea beans. It was simply that the red kidneys had more flavor.

"Light soil for the best-flavored beans," Father always said, and long before the word "conservation" became a catchall shibboleth, we did the plowing, harrowing, furrowing out in a rush. The purpose was to expose the soil of the furrow as brief a time as possible.

"Don't let the soil dry out and the beans will germinate faster and grow better," Father said. We furrowed out with Old Jerry and the one-horse plow. Well-rotted manure was scattered along the bottom of the furrow and two or three inches of soil pulled over the manure.

On commercial bean farms today, the seed is drilled in an evenly spaced line; but in 1910 we dropped the seeds in hills, four to a hill and the hills about two feet apart, and rows three feet apart. I cultivated with Old Jerry two or three times, and about the middle of July the rows were hilled up. That's all there was to it until late September or perhaps early October. Then it was stacking time.

Stacking wasn't too bad a task, even though I felt I should be exploring the woods or checking the porcupine ledges on the hill above the pasture spring. I cut a number of two- to three-inch-diameter gray birch trees and used the butt ends for the stacking poles. The butt was cleaned of branches for about two feet and the branches above were clipped off to leave stubs about ten inches long. The pole was perhaps seven or eight feet in length, and after a crowbar made a hole in the soft sandy loam, the pole was set in and a few old shingles or pieces of board placed around the butt.

If you have never stacked beans, it won't mean too much when I say that half an acre can grow a good many bean plants. You pulled a handful of the crisp, frost-blackened and shriveled plants, knocked the loose soil off against your leg, and then pushed the plants, root ends first, among the stubs of the pole. The idea was to keep the root ends higher than the leaves and pods so that rain would drain off. We hoped for dry weather, of course, and some seasons we could get the beans into the barn without their getting wet.

Looking back, half a century, I wonder why we let those bean stacks stand in the field for a fortnight or so after stacking. Probably Father felt the beans themselves were not sufficiently dried to go into the barn. Still, if memory serves, those plants and pods were brittle dry when they were pulled. Day after day, as soon as I got home from school, I changed into farm clothes and stacked beans until chore time. It was slow methodical work, and each stack had to be built carefully. This was one of the tasks for which I was paid cash money—10 cents an hour, as I recall. I am not certain whether a dime is a part of the monetary system today, or whether it begins with a quarter, but in those days a dime was a definite part of the economy.

After the beans were stacked and had dried in the field for a spell, Old Jerry and I hauled the stacks to the barn.

The plants were so tightly packed around the poles that you could pull the stack from its hole, get the tip end onto the floor of the farm cart, hoist the butt end, and shove the stack along the cart body. I took the stacks to the big barn and set them under the west scaffold to wait for that windy November or December day when we did the flailing. The rush and worry were over once the beans were under cover.

Unless you used to flail your own beans, I'll bet you've never heard of a stail, a toggle, and a swingle. A flail is used for pounding the beans from the brittle pods; it has a handle and a shorter piece that comes down flat on the spread-out beans. The stail is the handle, the swingle is the short piece that actually whacks the beans, and the toggle is the piece of leather or rope that fastens the stail to the swingle. Somewhere I have read that years ago the farmers along the Massachusetts coast used dried eels' skins for the thong connecting stail and swingle. Perhaps eel skin was especially tough and pliable.

Father and I enjoyed flailing beans on a December Saturday, after we were all caught up on our fall chores. I swept the barn floor and spread out the brittle dried beans with their long wrinkled pods in about a six- to eight-inch layer. Then Father and I went to work with our homemade flails. We were particular about our flails. Father used his flail for many years, but I made myself a new flail each year or two as I grew larger and stronger.

Flailing appeared to be a simple process, but actually it was a technique that had to be mastered. It was not difficult to lift the stail high, start the swing downward, and give yourself a solid painful crack on the head with the swingle. If you did it right, the swingle came down flat on the beans and the red kidneys popped into the air. When the mass had been worked over once, we fluffed it up with pitchforks and went over it a second time. Then the pods and broken vines were forked aside to be used as barn litter, and the beans, bits of vines and pods and dirt were swept into a pile.

I always enjoyed the winnowing, and since Father liked to finish up the job on the same day it started, we always chose a breezy December day. The beans and all the dirt and debris were shoveled into a battered old tin tub. Another old tub was set on the ground outside the door. We opened the big door at the other end of the barn driveway to insure a strong draft. The beans were poured from one tub to the other until the wind swept away all the extraneous material.

When it was all over, all the beans winnowed and poured into the three or four wooden buckets that sat under the bottom shelf in the pantry, Father always said the same thing: "There, that means we have our Saturday night suppers for another year."

I wish just once I could be ten years old again, kneeling contentedly beside the big shallow wooden tub in Johnson's Mill at the foot of schoolhouse hill. I would put one end of a long oat straw in my mouth, the other in the freshly pressed apple juice, and slowly, pleasantly, and completely tank up on the flavorful golden-amber liquid. Probably I shouldn't use the words "tank up," but when I think of the way a few of us boys took advantage of Mr. Johnson's generosity, that's the only phrase that adequately expresses the situation.

The old-fashioned cider mills are about gone. Today's process is a scientific one with power machinery doing the work; the bottling is often done mechanically and even the labels are pasted on by machine. It wouldn't be autumn in New England without rows of the appealing-colored liquid gleaming in the sunshine on hundreds of roadside stands. No doubt the modern product is excellent, but I wonder if it's any better than the cider I remember.

I am fully aware that apple juice should never be called "cider." At just what stage in its developing career the juice becomes cider, I would not pretend to know. I will admit that, when Father used to put down a few barrels of juice to become vinegar, I may have occasionally sampled the barrels just to see what the aging liquid tasted like. I like Webster's definition: "Cider—the expressed juice of apples, used for drinking and making cider. Cider that has fermented is called hard cider and contains 2 to 8 per cent alcohol." While we are on the subject, here is Webster's opinion of applejack: "Brandy distilled from cider; also a beverage produced by freezing hard cider." I have never heard of brandy distilled from cider, but there are intermittent rumors up here about certain citizens who freeze cider and siphon off the liquid that does not freeze in the center of a barrel.

In Johnson's Mill the apples were ground; then layers of the soft juicy material were put in the pressing box with strips of burlap between the layers. When the big pressing box was filled, the squeezing began. As I recall it, Mr. Johnson had two or three jacks that he turned with a stout pole. The jacks sat on a plank across the press and had a firm bearing against an overhead beam. The juice flowed and dripped into the large-diameter, shallow tub —the source of supply for boys who carefully collected long oat straws. When most of the juice was pressed out, the mill man took off the jack, removed the pulp layer by layer, and then refilled the press.

One of my jobs in the fall was to take loads of cider apples—sortings from the crop and fallen apples that I picked up under the trees—to Johnson's cider mill. And then one day Father bought a hand cider press at an auction for a dollar or two, and another chore was added to my list. It was my job to operate the press.

It was readily identifiable as the Standard Cider Mill in the mail-order catalog. On a heavy solid framework, the grinding box, powered by gears and a hand crank, crushed the apples which were fed into the top of the box. Beneath the grinding box was a slatted half tub which received the juicy, pulpy mass of ground apples. When this slatted tub was full, it was transferred to the other end of the platform, and the press screw with its wooden head was turned down to extract the last possible drop of juice. There were two of the slatted tubs. Thus while the pressure was on one, the other was receiving a fresh supply of ground-up apples. The platform on which the two tubs sat sloped toward the screw press end, and the brown-gold liquid ran from the platform to a wooden half tub on the floor.

The mail-order catalog was definite in its description, as it was about most of the farm equipment that was operated by boys. "You cannot buy an easier running, better finished, or stronger made hand cider mill at any price. The mill has a capacity of six to 12 barrels of cider per day." I did not attempt to prove or disprove the capacity—any more than I was tempted to see how much I could do with the one-hole corn sheller or the turnip slicer. I just worked along at *my* capacity. It wasn't the worst job in the world, and I always had a chance to "tank up." Hour after hour, I fed apples into the hopper, ground them up, transferred the dripping mass to the press side, turned down the press, ground more apples, and carried the fresh cider to the big wooden barrels in the cellar. Come summer, Father would have top-flight vinegar to sell. Mother and my sisters took some of the fresh-pressed juice to the house and boiled apple slices in it to make boiled-cider apple sauce. As I recall, she also boiled down some of the cider to a gooey consistency to use in cooking during the winter.

When good farmers got together in those days, there was always an interesting discussion about the apples that made the best cider.

Father wanted a certain mixture of varieties: Baldwins, Blue Pearmains, Roxbury Russets, Kings, and Sheep Noses to get just the blend of liquid goodness that he felt was the best. Other citizens had other opinions. Some of them made hard cider and even added raisins and brown sugar to increase the potency. There was one man who put down several barrels of cider which he announced he would sell as vinegar the following summer. But for some inexplicable reason he rarely had any vinegar to sell. He claimed that on his hillside farm, in the rarefied upland atmosphere, the cider evaporated before it had a

111

chance to turn.

Speaking of farm equipment that was usually operated by my muscles, I should describe the Acme One-Hole Corn Sheller. I don't know the exact origin of corn or maize, but I do know that this member of the grass family has played a starring role in the history of our country. Corn helped the early settlers through the first difficult years. When families left the coastal communities and pushed back toward the mountains, when they wound through the mountain passes and flatboated down the rivers to the heartland, they carried corn seed with them. As men cleared forest land in the North and Northeast, they planted precious kernels among the charred stumps that marked the beginning of farms. In thousands of log cabins, cornmeal mush was a staple food, supplemented with wild game.

Men carried bags of corn on their backs along woodland paths to the nearest gristmill. Along the first rough roads, by horseback and ox team, the corn was carried and the meal returned to lonely cabins in the clearings. Corn meant food for family and livestock. As the generations passed and the stone-free, fertile soil of the Midwest was put to the plow, more and more corn was raised. Livestock production increased and meat-processing companies started. Corn became a staple crop, a foundation of American farming. Today hybrid corn is grown on hundreds of thousands of acres—each stalk the same height, each stalk with the same number of ears. Powerful machines plow and harrow, plant the seeds, cultivate and harvest.

Half a century ago many farmers in the Northeast

still raised field corn from seed that had been passed down from father to son. Father was a staunch believer in raising all the food possible, both for the family and for the stock. I can recall that he told me about the history of corn. It never grows without men's aid, nor can it. Many farmers think it the most decorative of all crops. It was the botanist DeCandolle who wrote, "If ever a plant could be said to be devised for the use of man, that plant is Indian corn." Some of the names were musical and imaginative: Legal Tender, Shoe Peg, Upchurch Red, Bank Stock, Bonus Prairie, Bloody Butcher, Cranberry, Jersey Red, Big Buckeye, Scioto, Rhode Island White Crop, Kissing Cousin, King Philip, Angel of Midnight, Chittendon, Bird Track, Gold Drop, Blue Flint, Beer Yellow, and New Canaan.

For a few years after we came to Glenrose Farm, Father raised two or three acres of field corn. We planted by hand. As I remember, it was six kernels per hill, and the hills about three feet apart. "One kernel for the crows, one for the bugs, and four to grow" was a rural maxim. Old Jerry and I did most of the cultivating, and I trudged many a mile up and down the rows, hanging onto the handles of the cultivator. Old Jerry knew the job as well as I, and I simply tied the reins to the cultivator handles. At the end of each long row, he took a big circle so that we came straight into the next row. It was always a good day in July when we did the last cultivation and the corn was "laid by" to grow the rest of the season.

I did not mind the shocking too much, although it grew a bit tiresome. Late in the fall we hauled the shocks to the barn, and then came the part about the corn program that was a trial—the one-hole sheller. The mail-order catalog said that the Acme One-Holer was "guaranteed to give perfect satisfaction and do good work. Crank is on the right side making feeding convenient. Has a heavy balance wheel and is geared low so that it is easy to operate."

That last statement, as far as I was concerned, was a matter of opinion. In spite of the heavy balance wheel, it took a lot of muscle power to rip the kernels from the cobs. A husked cob was pushed into the hole in the top shelf. I turned the crank and the rag-iron pulled the kernels from the cob. A fan blew the debris away, and the shelled corn dropped into a tin tub beneath the center of the sheller. The cobs came out a hole in one end. It was, the catalog said, "the best value ever offered in a corn sheller," and the "most popular style hand corn sheller ever made." That may be, but I'm not sure how they determined it was the "lightest running corn sheller on the market."

Slicing turnips with the Peerless Root Cutter was not much better in my estimation. The turnip has a long horticultural history. The Romans were growing many kinds of turnips at the beginning of the Christian era; some of the names were of Greek origin, indicating that the turnip may have traveled westward. Pliny wrote about turnips in the first century. The turnip was brought to the New World by Jacques Cartier in 1541, and it was planted by the Virginian colonists in 1609. We grew a sizable patch of turnips on the farm for winter cattle feed, and one of my daily tasks when I arrived home from District School was to slice a few bushels in the

MEMORIES OF A COUNTRY BOYHOOD

Peerless Root Cutter.

The catalog description of the machine was glowing. "We make these machines with improvements that cannot be found in any other root cutters. They have the best steel-knives, easily taken out to sharpen and will last for years. The feed is cut fine to avoid all danger of choking. These machines are made of good-sized parts well bolted and screwed together, have a large hopper, well painted and ornamented and we guarantee them to be the best root cutters manufactured. Weight 140 pounds. Capacity by hand 30 to 50 bushels per hour. Price with crank, $7.25."

Regardless of what the catalog said, it was work enough to get four or five bushels from the big heap of turnips in the barn, carry them in a battered tin tub to the cutter, fill the hopper, and then turn the crank. As my arm began to ache, I remembered cultivating, hoeing, weeding, and thinning out the turnips on hot July days; I remembered the fall job of pulling the "Swedes" and then hauling them to the barn. As I watched the juicy slices drop into the tub, I knew I was finishing a task that had begun months before, and there was some consolation in that. "Nothing like turnip," my Grandfather used to say, "to keep the cows in good flesh and good production." He should have added that they kept small boys in good shape too.

Banking the house with sawdust was an annual task on Glenrose Farm. We had special equipment for it— long, fourteen-inch-wide hemlock boards and pointed oak stakes were kept at one end of the horse barn during the

115

summer. Come a pleasant day in late fall, the boards and stakes were set in place around the house.

Long before scientists began using various materials for insulation, pioneers and farmers had learned the cold-repelling, heat-holding qualities of sawdust. We banked the house with sawdust and I always anticipated the day when Father would say, "Haydn, better set up the boards today and take the mare in for a load or two of sawdust." After I set the stakes, I went to the barn and hitched up Belle to the big farm wagon with the high board sides.

I suppose that a lad gets an equal thrill from driving a truck today, but a truck cannot whinny a friendly greeting when you open the barn door. A truck cannot nuzzle a boy's overalls pocket for a sugar cookie that has been lifted from the cookie jar.

The plump horse was full of ginger as I drove to Johnson's sawmill. It was good to raise a hand in greeting to neighborhood farmers along the road and see them lift their arms in grave salute.

At the mill I met other lads who were filling carts from the big sawdust pile. It wasn't hard work to shovel the cart full—much easier than loading dressing and spreading it on the fields. We listened to the men swap stories, and if the cider press was in operation Mr. Johnson did not object if boys took oat straws and tanked up on the cold amber liquid.

It took two loads of sawdust to fill the trough around the house, with a little left over for bedding the calf pens. Naturally, when I got back with the last load, the first thing to do was to see how Mother was coming along with the Saturday baking. As Father always said when he helped himself to a handful of cookies or a fat applesauce turnover, "Son, in spite of what they say, womenfolk are always glad to see their men enjoy their cooking."

By the time I'd filled the trough and put the balance of the sawdust in the barn, day was ending. The Morgan was glad to get to her stall, and the cows and neatstock were calling for their hay. Not a very exciting chore, perhaps, but somehow I remember feeling a sense of satisfaction as one more job was completed in getting ready for a northland winter.

CHAPTER FOUR

A KITCHEN should be the heart of a home. It should be spacious and have an old red-cherry drop-leaf table where a woman prepares food. The eating table should have a red and white checked cloth; the brass-bowled coal-oil lamp should be on an extension chain. Red geraniums should be blossoming in the south windows; the big wood-burning stove should be gleaming bright, with a warming oven above and a reservoir for hot water at the rear. In the evening a man should sit in a comfortable chair with his feet on the ledge of the open oven. And there should be plenty of kindling ready to start the fire in the morning.

It could be that electricity and gas are to blame for much of the jitteriness that distinguishes our social order. Too many ladies push buttons, pull levers, twirl dials, twist knobs, set alarm clocks, and then leave home. Nature never intended a person to put a roast in an oven at 9:45 A.M., leave it set for a spell, start cooking by itself at 2:59, and turn itself off at 5:47. And if that isn't bad enough, they have invented a steam pressure cooker that will half cook and half frighten good grub into abject submission in two or three minutes. It means, in effect, that a lady can be running around all day, get home a few minutes before six, and then shoot a meal onto the table in eight and a half minutes flat.

I suppose, basically, the thing that's wrong is the modern kitchen. Modern kitchens are white, gleaming, antiseptic places with floors that show the dirt easily, and half a mile of counter space, more or less, that has to be kept clean. The modern stove is the worst of all—a white contraption with gongs, cymbals, bells, time bombs, complex gears, starters, stoppers, speeder-uppers, and slower-downers. I'm against it. That's no way to cook, not when you could have an Acme Triumph Six Hole Blue Polished Steel Range.

Mother had struggled along with our old stove for years. It was a good baker, and she turned out bread and biscuits, pies and cakes and puddings for the family. The squat, six-quart iron kettle with its stubby legs often sat in a cover hole and simmered mouth-watering stews, soups, and chowders. But the old stove had done its duty; it was time for a new one. Mother sat right down and ordered an Acme Six Holer.

It was a magnificent stove. The mail-order catalog description was specific and enthusiastic. "Unconditionally guaranteed the best looking, the best cooking, the best baking range made in the world. Plain smooth castings, will not catch or hold dirt. You can't judge a range until you have tried it. We allow you to try this range at home for 60 days. If it is not beyond question of doubt the best baker and the best fuel saver you have ever seen, you may return the range at our expense."

The body was "built like a boiler," made of Wellsville blue polished steel. The warming closet upstairs extended the length of all six stove covers. "Just the proper height for the average person." The oven was 20 by 21 by 14 and "has been constructed with great care and intelligence." The white porcelain-lined reservoir held 22 quarts and there was a damper beneath it, so that the heat could be regulated. The fire box was 27 inches long, ten inches wide, and eight inches deep. The entire top of the stove was 50 by 29 inches. There was plenty of nickel-plated trimming to set off the blue-black, highly polished steel.

That was a stove. It arrived by freight in a big planked crate and was moved on rollers from freight car to freight shed and then slid down planks to the two-horse sled. We rolled it from the sled to the back room, uncrated it, and then moved it on rollers to its home in our kitchen. From that moment on, the Acme Six Holer played a very important role in our lives. It heated the kitchen and it cooked and baked our food. Mother always kept a tea-kettle on the stove, and on a winter evening that kettle sang and chuckled above the crackling fire.

Mother baked big brown-crusted loaves of homemade bread in the oven, and I can still smell the marvelous fragrance as she turned the hot loaves out on the kitchen table. On top of the stove she made doughnuts, fried pancakes, and warmed up potatoes and gravy for supper. In that heavy iron kettle she made delicious beef stews, tomato chowders, and dumplings. On a winter's evening we sometimes had hot hulled corn in milk when the hulled corn man from Antrim came along with his products.

There were several other advantages to our Acme Six Holer. I admit, of course, that its primary function was to cook and bake; but on the farm it had other important points too. Behind the stove was a small rope line where men and boys could hang wet felt leggings and socks to dry in the evening. After a day's chopping in the wood lot in wet snow, leggings needed to dry out overnight. Sometimes overalls and pants needed a few hours of heat. The big white-lined reservoir was a help come Saturday evening when water was needed for the old tin tub in which

121

a lad took his weekly bath. Father believed in a moist warm mash for the hens once a day in winter, and hot water from the reservoir or the copper-bottomed teakettle was used to heat and moisten the ground oats and corn-meal.

Even Shep, our collie, was fond of that stove. He stretched out behind it and made little whimpering noises as he dreamed of the woodchuck in the garden wall. The two cats dozed on the braided rug. There was something friendly and personal about our stove. It had only one dis-advantage that I can think of. It required an unconscion-able amount of wood, and my sisters were always quick to remind me when the wood box was empty.

Stoves and kettles go together in my mind, and I can never think about one without thinking about the other. I well remember Mother's cherished iron stove kettle. I think many people called them "stove pots." This type of kettle sat in a stove cover hole directly above the flames. My recollection is that Mother's kettle held about six quarts. In it she made stews and chowders, and when I reached home from school about half-past four, the fra-grance from beef stews, corn chowder, or tomato chowder was so upsetting that I needed a few cookies or raspberry tarts before starting evening chores.

I dimly recall another iron kettle that Mother used oc-casionally. It was called, I think, a Scotch bowl. It was a shallow kettle with a handle, possibly a foot in diameter and about five inches deep. I don't recall what was cooked in this. Doesn't seem as though it would hold enough to feed two adults and four growing children with hearty appetites.

I remember the kettle that hung in the back yard a little better. Father had set two oaken posts about eight feet apart. A crossbar was spiked to the two tops, and a strong chain with a hook hung from the crossbar. The hook took the handle of the big soot-bottomed kettle. It was one of my tasks as soon as I arrived home from school to start a fire beneath the kettle. I cooked up small potatoes, pumpkins, squash, turnips, and potato peelings for the pigs. During the last half hour of cooking I added cornmeal. Father believed that cooked food meant a better flavor in hams and bacon. I can still see that old black kettle and the orange-red flames silhouetted against the dusk. And I can smell the pungent odor of the cooking food.

The copper kettle in the summer-kitchen brick arch was probably a fifty-gallon affair, and in it we heated water to scald the hogs at butchering time. Time plays tricks with memory, but I think Mother sometimes used that kettle to boil blankets, sheets, and perhaps other washables. Usually the clothes were boiled in a tin boiler that sat across two of the covers of the wood-burning stove, and we used a short-forked stick to wind up the wet hot clothes and transfer them to the tin wash tub.

The copper kettle in the arch was also used to boil down sap in the spring. Old Jerry and I brought in the sap in a big barrel on the farm sled. Then I dipped out the sap by pailfuls and poured it into the arch kettle. Mother took care of the boiling down, but I always hung around just in case she asked me to take a taste or two.

I've been told that the kitchen is supposed to be the province of womenfolk and girls, but it seems to me I spent an awful lot of time in our kitchen doing one chore or another. I didn't mind too much; at least I was close to the food supply, and I was never too busy to steal a cookie or offer my services as an official taster. Of course, there were times when I wanted to be somewhere else— and one of them was churning time.

"Churning's good for a boy," Father used to say with hearty emphasis and a genial smile. "Builds character."

I was not too concerned with my character on a spring Saturday morning when the sun was shining and the speckled trout in the meadow brook were flashing jewel colors as they darted through the shallows. But Mother was justifiably proud of her golden pound prints of butter with a four-leaf-clover design, and I guess I had to do my share.

The rich milk from the Guernseys was strained into round tin pans and a day later the thick covering of cream was taken off with a skimmer. The skimmer was shaped like a large clam shell and had many small holes through which milk drained away from the cream. The cream was carefully "ripened" and on churning day was often set behind the stove to warm. As I poured the cream into the churn, there was always one question uppermost in my mind: would the butter "come" easily and quickly, or would I have to keep on turning the crank forever.

Over the years men have tried many types of churns and contrived various gadgets. The common dash churn of colonial days was a tall slender wooden cask. A long handle went through the cover at the top, and you worked the handle straight up and down. Pioneers also used a rocker churn—a rectangular box on a frame set on two rockers. The churner grasped a knob and rocked the box back and forth. Half a century ago, the Union churn was popular in certain regions. It resembled a barrel cut longitudinally and had a hinged cover. It stood on four sturdy wooden legs and came in sizes that held from five to twelve gallons of cream. It featured gear wheels which were supposed to make the turning easy.

But on Glenrose Farm we used a white cedar cylinder churn with a double dasher. The advertisement in the catalog said, "The crank is locked to the churn with a clamp and thumbscrew, which prevents leakage. The best churn in use." That may be, but as I worked along, trickles of cream oozed out around the crank.

At first, the dashers went slopping through the warm cream in a loose easy way. It was heavy liquid, but it was still a liquid. Round and round I turned the crank. Sometimes I could induce a sister to turn the crank for a few minutes while I took some needed nourishment. But on Glenrose Farm churning was a boy's job. Sometimes the butter "came" surprisingly quickly—and it always happened on a day when I wasn't in much of a hurry to attend to vital matters. On a day, however, when I desperately needed to explore a woodland, go fishing, or check on a fox's den, the churning kept on and on and on.

I listened anxiously for a change in the sound. By the time I had turned the crank for half an hour my arm was aching. And still the cream went ker-slop, ker-slop, loose and easy. A half an hour is a gargantuan length of time on a day when the outdoors is calling. Then came that wonderful moment. The fat globules began to coagulate into chunks of butter and the tune changed to a lower, deeper song as the big blobs of butter fell from the top paddle into the buttermilk.

Mother gave the crank a turn or two. "It's come," she said. "Thank you, Haydn. I hope you'll catch us a nice mess of trout."

Making ice cream was a tiresome job too; but somehow I didn't mind it as much as churning, probably because the rewards were a little better. Father liked ice cream as much as I did, and we were the proud owners of a White Mountain Ice Cream Freezer.

In those days the White Mountain Freezer Company of Nashua, New Hampshire, did a big business, and in one of their early catalogs they described the freezer: "The White Mountain Freezer is so unusually popular with the trade and consumer alike, and its merits so well known the world over, that a review of its many features of superiority seems unnecessary.

"It is a strong, waterproof tub, bound with heavy, galvanized hoops; the gearing completely covered so that nothing can get between the cogs. Cans are full size and made of the very best quality of tin plate; beaters are made of malleable iron and tinned. All castings are nicely galvanized to prevent rusting.

"It is the only Freezer in the world having the triple motion, three simultaneous motions, whereby the cream is beaten more thoroughly during the process of freezing. Above all, remember that all surfaces of the White Mountain Freezer that come in contact with the cream are tinned, therefore there is no danger of zinc poisoning. Will

126

freeze in half the time of any other freezer and produce cream of the finest quality."

No one knows precisely when ice cream was invented, but we know that Emperor Nero enjoyed flavored snow. We know that Marco Polo brought a recipe from China that was similar to our modern sherbet. According to a Vermont Extension Service release, "It is reported that Charles the First gave his French chef a lifetime pension in exchange for a promise that his ice cream should never be served anywhere except at the royal table."

Apparently it was an American housewife, Nancy Johnson, who set up the first contraption that resembled the familiar homemade freezer. She devised a workable tub, gears, and a crank. The first commercial venture was started in 1851 by Jacob Fussell of Baltimore. The second plant was started in Washington, D.C., and the third plant in Boston in 1862. As far as I know the first newspaper advertisement for ice cream appeared on May 19, 1777, in the New York *Gazette*. The first patent on a freezer was issued in 1848. At one time there was a great to-do as to whether the dasher should revolve inside the container or whether the container should revolve around a stationary dasher.

Those were points that did not concern me. On a hot summer day, along about four o'clock in the afternoon, I hoped Father would say, "Haydn, why don't you call it enough for today and see if Mother will mix us up a batch of ice cream?" While Mother mixed the cream, eggs, sugar, and flavorings, it was my task to get the ice and to pound it fine. The icehouse with its big trough was near the milk house; part of the trough was in the milk house, and in it we chilled the milk with cakes of ice.

I dug out a cake of ice and pulled it over to the trough and sloshed off the sawdust. Usually some of the sawdust stuck to the ice, so I had a stub of a house broom that I kept in the milk house to wash the ice cake clean. With an old axe I cut the big cake into four or five chunks and put them into a cornmeal bag. In those days a cornmeal bag was made of heavy cloth compared to the material used for bran and ground oats. Then I used the flat side of the axe head to pound the ice into small pieces which could be packed around the can in which the cream was frozen.

We had a six-quart freezer and it required a sizable supply of ice. I set the freezer on a wheelbarrow at the back door of the woodshed, where I could work in the shade. Mother poured the rich yellow mixture into the can. Then I packed the freezer with alternate layers of ice and salt. I am not a chemist, but as I understand it the salt melts the ice and the melting ice freezes the cream. I started the cranking job with considerable enthusiasm. Naturally I operated the ice-cream freezer with a happier heart than I cranked the grindstone or the churn.

The first five minutes were easy. The crank turned smoothly and one could hear the light slosh-sloshing of the liquid as the wooden paddles went round and round. From time to time I used a small stick to tamp down the ice; then I added more ice and salt around the metal can. Sometimes I could bribe one of my sisters to turn for a few minutes, but usually my sisters adopted a superior attitude when I proposed anything that meant work for them. By and by, perhaps in ten or fifteen minutes, I could feel the mixture starting to harden. I kept turning steadily, even

if my arm muscles began to feel it. And when the job was almost done, Father would appear and say, "Haydn, let me give it a few more turns." Then came the happy moment. "I guess we'll call it done," he would say.

We had a family tradition on Glenrose Farm concerning the ice cream. When it was done, Father carefully cleaned off the ice and salt, lifted the cover, and slowly pulled out the dasher. While the rest of the family had small saucerfuls, I had the dasher to lick, and Father was always generous in the amount he left on the paddles. Then the can was covered and packed to wait for supper.

The kitchen was probably the busiest place on Glenrose Farm, what with Mother and my three sisters in there most of the time, and Father and myself making periodic visits just to see what was going on. Saturday was baking day, and you never saw such activity. Mother made pies and bread, cookies, cakes, and turnovers. She just couldn't face the world unless she could offer friends at least three choices of cake. We got up early on Saturday so that Mother would have a long forenoon, and as I recall we often had a beef stew for Saturday dinner so that the oven would be free for the baking.

I often wondered how Mother did so many things so efficiently. In one forenoon she baked pies, cookies, and cakes. And she made large, light, golden doughnuts. Hot from the fat, they were delicious, but I don't know that I would rate them above apple turnovers or oatmeal cookies studded with raisins. That was one pleasant thing about baking day. Usually I didn't have to make decisions; I was willing to eat a sample of everything.

130

I was not interested in baking and cooking as such. No reason why I should be. I was blessed with three able sisters. Their mission in life was to help Mother and to keep me out of the kitchen except when the wood box was low. Another one of their self-assigned missions was to prevent me from getting the cookies, doughnuts, turnovers, and other food I needed between meals—as well as a snack or two for Old Jerry. On a good Saturday when Father had outlined some tasks, I needed refueling frequently. Whether I was stacking beans, getting in rowen, working in the orchard, or wheeling in wood and stacking tiers in the woodshed, I felt impelled to go to the kitchen often to see how Mother was making out. If the kitchen windows were open and the door from the kitchen to the back room was ajar, the tantalizing fragrance of Saturday baking floated out to the woodshed and to the yard. As soon as I smelled that odor, I headed straight for the kitchen. And it took more than my three sisters to keep me out.

Apple butter time was an annual kitchen event. One Saturday morning along about the eleventh month, Mother would announce at breakfast, "Children, we'll make apple butter today."

Father had little to do with apple butter making, but he was much interested in apple flavors and over the years he and Mother conducted experiments. Our apple butter was a mixture, and I remember the Snow apples, Blue Pearmains, Baldwins, and Northern Spies that we used. There were other varieties, of course—Golden Russet, Tolman Sweets, Sheepsnose, Yellow Bellflower, Pumpkin Sweet, Seek-No-Further, Missing Link, Pine Stump, Plumb Cider, Hoary Morning, Cathead, Irish Peach, Pound Sweeting,

131

Chenango Strawberry, Winter Cheese, Red Horse, Garden Royal, Orange Sweeting, just to name a few. But after a time Father devised our mixture, and as far as I was concerned it was the best.

I had two opinions about apple butter making. There was no question that it was better than cleaning out calf pens or hauling barnyard dressing to the fields. On the other hand, it became mighty monotonous work before the November sun sank behind Ball Mountain and the shadows made night camps in the valleys and woodlands. It was a long drawn-out job. The first part was not so bad. I sat at the drop-leaf cherry table in the kitchen and used the Goodell Apple Parer. Each apple was pushed onto the two sharp-pointed steel prongs and then the crank turned the apples against a sharp blade. Long colorful peelings reeled off and my sisters tossed the ribbons of peel over their shoulders to see if they would form the initials of the Prince Charming who would come into their lives.

While the girls quartered and cored the apples, it was my task to set up the shining copper kettle in the back yard beneath the big plum tree and build a fire under it. Then sweet cider was poured in the kettle and simmered down to the right consistency. The apples were put into the cider and the real work began; for Mother insisted that the brown, bubbling mass be stirred constantly. We had a long, specially shaped paddle that Father had made from a crooked tree limb. I can still see that brown-stained paddle—a peeled, crooked affair, flattened at the kettle end, rounded for the handle end.

The stirring was my job, but from time to time I got a few minutes' relief from one of my sisters when I claimed that the fire needed attention. Naturally the fire had to be looked after frequently. Mother was very particular about her apple butter and had a reputation for its flavor and quality. It was an art to keep the fire going just right with pieces of maple, oak, and ash. And of course, after the apple butter making was under way, Mother had her regular Saturday baking to do and a fellow needed a drink of water and a chance to see how the cookies were coming along.

Hour after hour the process went on. Toward late afternoon I could feel the mass of glistening brown material begin to thicken. Then Mother added the spices from her cherished secret recipe that had come down through her family—cinnamon, allspice, nutmeg, and ginger and cloves. The hot bubbling apple butter gave off a wonderful fragrance. You could inhale that spicy odor all over the yard. From time to time Father came along to take a look—and a taste. Mother tasted and tasted. We all had samples on big soda crackers. "A dite more cloves, Mother," Father would say, or, "Just a little more cinnamon." It would be dusk in the valley and sunset would be flaming on the mountain top before Mother would finally say, "There, that's just right. Haydn, put out the fire." We knew we had a supply of apple butter for another year.

Sausage making was another kitchen chore of mine. It seems to me I was always cranking or stirring something; and when sausage-making time came around every winter, it was my arm that operated the meat grinder.

Every year we raised a couple of pigs for family meat. With a family of four growing children, Father and Mother planned to produce all the home-grown food they could.

We butchered at the end of December or in early January. We wanted to be sure that winter had set in for keeps, for fresh pork was a major item in our winter diet. It was easy to pickle and smoke the ham and bacon so that they would keep without trouble, but fresh pork was a different proposition. I can remember how good fresh pork liver was—fried in a big iron spider on top of the gleaming Acme Six Holer. Fresh tender liver and creamy mashed potatoes flavored with the liver drippings was one of Mother's meals I always looked forward to.

Sausage making was a Saturday job and one that I was happy to participate in, for a self-evident reason. Mother was a master hand at the process, but she was always glad to have Father's opinion as to the seasoning. That meant she fried many small "tasting" patties before the bulk was pushed tightly into the cloth bags. When I had finished my work at the meat grinder, putting through the lean and fat, I hung around until Mother was ready to fry the sample patties. We all stood around as the small round cakes sputtered on the stove. Then we sampled. I don't think that my opinion, or that of my three sisters, was especially helpful, but we all waited for Father's verdict.

Father was a moderate man, and he didn't hurry. "Slow and steady" was his motto for work. He would take his patty on a small plate, cut a piece with his fork, and put it into his mouth. He enjoyed the sampling process as much as we did. Without a trace of a smile, he would look at me, look at my sisters, and finally say, "Rosie, that's good. That's very good. But don't you think it could stand just a bit more salt?"

What a relief! That meant that Mother would work in

134

a little more salt, or what ever Father thought it needed; and then she would fry another round of patties for us. A mid-morning lunch of sausage, plus perhaps a few cookies and a glass of milk, was an excellent reward for turning the grinder.

Our farm cellar was a wonderful place. All summer long Mother canned and preserved. There was a long wide shelf, suspended from the floor timbers, that ran most of the length of the cellar. On this were jars of colorful cherries, blueberries, and raspberries. There were jars of string beans, peas, and corn. In cupboards along the south wall were scores of jars of jellies and jams, pickles and preserved plums. When you went downstairs to the cellar, the colors of the fruits and jellies made an appealing picture in the golden lantern light.

In the brick archway that formed the foundation for the big chimney and meant fireplaces on both the first floor and the second, we stored the winter supply of potatoes— smooth mealy Green Mountains and chunky Irish Cobblers. There were boxes of carrots and beets, stored in clean fresh sand; and on a plank platform, a heap of yellow rutabagas and a barrel or two of hard-headed winter cabbage. At one end of the cellar on a wooden platform were boxes of carefully selected Northern Spies, Baldwins, Russets, and Rhode Island Greenings.

Apples were the standard fruit for our family—from the first Astrakans in late July until the last of the long-keeping varieties the following April. Father always had a few boxes of fancy apples that he cherished for winter evenings. He would go down cellar, get a big yellow bowlful, peel them, and pass quarters to us on the end of his pocket knife. The cooking apples were in barrels, and Father and Mother always argued pleasantly over the technique of using them. Mother believed in using up those with bad spots first. "Rosie," Father would say, "you're always using poor apples by your method. Throw out the poor ones and just use the good ones." But Mother's thrifty habits compelled her to use up the ones that had started to go bad.

I remember big earthen jars of water glass in which we stored eggs. In those days hens did not have heated apartments, running water, ultraviolet rays, and scientifically balanced rations that compelled them to lay eggs in the late fall and early winter. We didn't expect eggs until toward the end of February, when the cheerful cackle of the birds fitted well with the climbing sun and pleasant hint of winter's end.

After butchering, we had a big barrel filled with salt pork—salt pork that was carefully selected for its amount of lean. One of Father's dictums was that you could not have topflight baked beans unless the pork was at least a third lean. I remember going downstairs for Mother, taking off that round wooden cover with a stone for weight, and fishing in the cold crackling brine for a chunk of the pork.

The smells and fragrances of our cellar are difficult to describe. Probably it was the cool moisture of the cellar that accentuated the odors, but the minute you opened the cellar door and started down the worn stairs, you could inhale that earthy smell that is duplicated nowhere else in the world.

I can still see the colorful jars of pickles in the cupboard against the far wall of the cellar. Mother was particularly proud of her pickles, relishes, and chutneys, and I was particularly fond of pickles in any shape or form. The cupboard was full of pickled beets, corn relish, green tomato chutney, corn and pepper relish, pickled pears, pickled cucumbers, piccalilli, pickled cherries, tomato and apple relish, green apple chutney, Nine Day peach pickles, chili sauce, watermelon pickle, and beet and onion pickle. And there were, of course, the standard sweet pickles that we ate with meats, hash, and baked beans. There were the dill pickles too. I preferred the sweet pickles myself and didn't go for a pickle that puckered all the way down. Mother's pickled crab apples were a special favorite. They were beautifully colored miniature apples, pickled in a just-right brine, and each apple with its stem so you could manipulate it in accord with the tenets of gracious living.

No one knows when pickles came into the human diet, but it was long, long ago. Caesar insisted that his soldiers have pickles on their long marches; Cleopatra thought they were a beauty adjunct; and Elizabeth I considered them a delicacy. Thomas Jefferson wrote, "On a hot day in Virginia, I know of nothing more comforting than a fine, spiced pickle, brought up trout-like from the sparkling depths of that aromatic jar below stairs in Aunt Sally's cellar."

The best pickle? A decision is difficult, but the one pickle that I would choose if cast on a desert island would be Mother Elliott's bread 'n' butter. This is a sweet-tart pickle that goes superbly well with meats and hashes, salads and baked beans. Mother used to make it and I still remember the recipe. Use six quarts of green cucumbers, sliced as

137

for table use and with the skins left on, one quart of onions sliced one-quarter inch thick, and two sweet red peppers cut into small pieces. Put the cucumbers, onions, and peppers in an enamel pan and sprinkle with one half cup of salt. Cover and let stand overnight; in the morning drain off the liquid.

In another pan put one quart of vinegar, eight cups of sugar, one dozen whole cloves, one and a half teaspoons of turmeric, and one and a half teaspoons of celery seed. Bring this to a boil and add cucumbers, onions, and peppers. Boil for seven minutes. Then put in jars immediately and seal.

While I'm on the subject of food, I might as well tell you where I stand on the issue of pumpkins versus squash. I am glad that John Greenleaf Whittier was one of my ancestors, for he was a good solid, sensible poet, and it was he who asked, "What calls back the past like the rich pumpkin pie?"

Come fall on Glenrose Farm there were always piles of golden pumpkins and heaps of colorful squashes against the south side of the old weathered barn. As soon as the first frost blackened the leaves, we gathered the fruits from the fields and heaped them up to ripen a week or two before they were stored away for fall and winter use. On cold nights the heaps were covered with old horse blankets, worn-out patchwork quilts, and moth-eaten buffalo robes that Mother donated for farm purposes. Some of the pumpkins went to the warm attic to be stored with squashes and onions near the chimney; and some of them were sliced and fed to the cows. But Mother always selected a few perfect ones for pie, and I was happy to help her carry them in to the kitchen. There are various, commendable uses for *Cucurbita pepo,* the pumpkin, and for *Cucurbita maxima,* the squash. But the best destiny for either pumpkin or squash is in a correctly concocted pie with plenty of spices, sugar, and cream, held in position by a flaky crust. Now squash pie is all right, but pumpkin pie has always been my favorite.

The history of the cucurbita goes far back. Evidence points to tropical America as the place of origin, and probably the history of squash and pumpkins is as old as the history of maize. Old-time names include maycoch, askutasquash, quaasien, ecushaws, and simmels. We know from explorers' journals that North American Indians grew and dried both pumpkins and squash. We know that early settlers learned to grow these crops in their fields of corn. Half a century ago it was a common practice to plant a seed of pumpkin in a hill of corn.

139

Farmers developed specific strains and gave musical names to the varieties that were passed along from father to son. Some old squash names are Heart O'Gold, Possum Nose, Winnebago, Chirimen, Mohawk Valley Giant, Arikara, Yellow Monster, and Valparaiso Cheese. Pumpkin names include Boston Pie, Big Chance, Quaker Pie, Yellow Sugar, Boston Greek, Chinese Alphabet, Dunkhard, Michigan Mammoth, Nantucket Pie, Yum Yum, Bugle Gramma, and Patagonia.

An unbiased observer will agree that pumpkin names are a bit more colorful than the squash names, and that advantage carries over into the end product. It is difficult to explain to a layman, for example, the difference between highbush and lowbush blueberries. The former has just a whittle more flavor, a dite of sweet tanginess that the lowbush lacks. By the same token, it is just as hard to convince New Yorkers that honest clam chowder never has tomatoes. A clam chowder with tomatoes is an abomination to those who best know this product of the sea. But if you are experimental-minded and willing to judge objectively, a comparison of pumpkin and squash pies will inevitably lead to placing the pumpkin above the squash. This is not to say that a good squash pie is not a pleasant affair. A man can make do very well on a wedge or two of squash pie— if pumpkin is not available.

In the February 1838 issue of *The Cultivator* published in Albany, New York, there is a piece about pumpkin pie, written by a Solon Robinson of Iowa. He writes, "As economy IN the house is the active partner of industry OUT of the house, I will add one more to your valuable list of cooking recipes, though perhaps it is out of character for

140

a Hoosier to tell a Yankee how to make a pumpkin pie.

"Grease the pie plate evenly and well, and sift dry corn meal about as thick as you would make a pie crust evenly over it, and then spread the prepared pumpkin over the meal crust, bake in the usual way, eat it warm and before it is many days old. Be assured that such a pie is truly good, rich, healthy and economical."

I agree with Mr. Robinson. I can still taste Mother's pumpkin pie. She brought it to the table hot, covered over with thick fresh cream. It was a special treat, but we were always careful to save a little for breakfast the next morning.

Another one of Mother's special treats was salt codfish. We had salt codfish frequently in the summer. In the winter, after butchering, we had plenty of fresh pork and beef. But about once a fortnight Father would say, "Rosie, isn't it time for a salt-fish dinner?"

It may be, as some authorities claim, that the cod is low on the social scale compared with mackerel, halibut, and swordfish. I don't know all the details, but cod played an important role in the early years of our continent's development. When John Cabot discovered Nova Scotia in 1497, it is recorded that cod were so dense in the water that his men simply lowered baskets and hauled up the fish.

Cod are called ground fish. In the summer as the ocean water warms, the fish are sometimes found at a depth of 1500 feet. A cod will never take a beauty prize. Many species of fish have distinctive colorings and shapes, but the cod is plain and plebeian. In spite of the depth of water in which it lives, cod liver is rich in vitamin D, sometimes known as the "sunshine" vitamin.

141

Salt codfish was always welcome for Saturday noon dinner. We knew we would have baked kidney beans, Mother's famous brown bread, pickles and probably apple pie for supper. But if Father and I had spent a long forenoon in the woods, cutting pine and hemlock for lumber, or chopping hardwood for next winter's fuel, we wanted a dinner at noon—not a lunch.

I don't recall all the details, but I know the basic tenets. The fish was soaked in cold water overnight to reduce the saltiness. There was a creamy milk sauce with a chopped hard-boiled egg or two mixed in. Then, in addition, for that extra touch of goodness, Mother fried some salt pork which had been cut into small cubes. These salt-pork bits were golden brown and very crisp. All the pork scraps and some of the pork fat went into the cream sauce. Mother's sauce was thick and there was plenty of fish. The rivulets of golden fat on the creamy sauce plus the brown bits of crisp pork were a mouth-watering combination. We all heaped the sauce over a boiled Green Mountain or two and had a feast.

As I remember, the kitchen on Glenrose Farm was the busiest around Thanksgiving Day, and preparations always began well in advance. Instead of a turkey, we had a specially fattened Barred Plymouth Rock rooster. Each year about the first of November, Father chose a few of the biggest, plumpest roosters and put them in a special pen. This meant roasters for us over a period, but the biggest and best of all was tagged for the Thanksgiving feast. These birds were fed a special fattening diet of corn and whole wheat. A couple of days before Thanksgiving, the big chunky bird was prepared and hung in the cool cellar. That was really all that Father and I had to do with the preparations. When it came to cooking, Mother and my three sisters didn't want their menfolk underfoot.

I still don't understand why womenfolk have to wash curtains and clean cupboards before an event such as this; but as I grow older I find there are more and more things I don't comprehend. For about three days ahead of time the house was in organized turmoil. I am not certain of this point, but I think half a century ago Thanksgiving week was a vacation and boys and girls did not tramp the road to District School. There were enough outside chores to keep Father and me busy getting ready for the winter months, while inside Mother and my sisters whipped themselves into a frenzy.

It was traditional for us to have red-flannel hash for supper the day before Thanksgiving—not the miscellaneous mixture of canned beef, turnips, carrots, potatoes, and cabbage that so many erroneously label red flannel. That combination is calico hash. The genuine, original red flannel is 85 per cent cooked chopped beets, 12 per cent cooked chopped potatoes, and 3 per cent onions. The mixture is fried in bacon fat, and it doesn't hurt to have some pieces of lean bacon in the hash. That brings it to a little over 100 per cent, but it is a minor point.

Naturally, as the pantry shelves filled with mince, apple, and squash pies, along with several kinds of turnovers and cookies, a lad who was keeping an eye on things could do all right. Furthermore, it was fair pay for keeping the wood box filled. There were bowls of cranberry sauce, dishes of bread 'n' butter pickles, and I can still see that huge white platter covered with lilies—pieces of thin golden sponge cake held together with toothpicks so that they looked like a lily blossom. On Thanksgiving morning, one of the girls filled the lilies with whipped cream.

On the morning of the big day, the family was up early and the kitchen was a bustling spot. I have now learned not to eat ahead of a meal, but in 1910 I couldn't see that eating ahead reduced my appetite. It merely decreased my capacity. My sisters were so busy that I could get cookies, turnovers, and a lily or two without much difficulty; but I had in mind the roast chicken and the possibility of a drumstick. I liked all kinds of pies, and Mother always had one of her famous three-layer chocolate cakes with thick frosting between the layers and droozling down the sides. I don't suppose you could call it a moral problem; it transcended the ordinary level of ethics. It was what Father would call a question of will power. In fact he had a good sermon on the subject. He didn't think much of folks who had no will power, and on Thanksgiving morning I'm afraid that I was one of them.

The hour before the feast was a hard one. The menfolk, uncles and cousins, sat in the living room, while all the women were in the kitchen. You could smell the wonderful fragrance of the golden-brown roaster all through the house. Then Mother came to the door. "Dinner is ready," she said. Father asked the blessing and he made it short, but deep in our hearts we all felt the gratitude that he expressed for the good things of life, for friends and loved ones, for the chance to break bread together, and for the opportunity to live in this land where men knew freedom and could worship as conscience dictated.

It was a long, leisurely, happy meal. The food was delicious and boys and girls all wanted seconds. It was a feast —the annual feast that has become a part of our national tradition. But I know now that it was more than the good things we had to eat. It was the love and unity of family and the once a year reunion with loved ones.

CHAPTER FIVE

THERE are, among many, three pictures I enjoy in the springtime of the year. One of them is a casually scattered bed of pink lady's-slippers in a woodland glade, where sun shafts slant through and outline shadow patterns from boles and limbs.

There are seven kinds of hardy orchids in the Northeast, and while I am no authority on the orchid family, I have never seen cultivated ones that appealed to me as do the wild ones. The pink lady's-slipper has two leaves that grow from the ground; there are no leaves on the stem. Somewhere I have read that this beautiful flower, sometimes called "whippoorwill's shoes," prefers light sandy soil; but looking back over the years I cannot recall seeing it except in woodlands where the soil is black and rich with accumulated humus. I have read that in colonial days there were patches of the flower covering many acres.

146

The fate of the pink lady's-slipper—and the fate of other wild flowers, makes me think of that biting phrase "destructively appreciated." Thoughtless persons rip and tear our wild flowers, and year by year the plants grow fewer. Perhaps Nature is partially responsible for the decrease of this flower. The stamens are in back of the pistil so that the vital pollen cannot be transferred except by an outside force. A bee crowds in for a sip of nectar; in leaving it creeps under an anther that almost blocks the path outward. The anther is loaded with pollen. The bee gets a covering of the pollen grains and goes to another slipper. Now, as it goes down for the nectar it is forced to go by a stigma of a pistil, and thus cross-fertilization is assured. It is a complicated system, and because of the unusual arrangement of stamens and pistils, many times the cross-fertilization fails. Thus it comes about that the plant often depends on root propagation, which is slow and perhaps uncertain.

A second woodland painting I enjoy is the time of golden candles on the pines. The experts tell us our evergreens are a living drawbridge, connecting the present with an ancient epoch when a vast evergreen belt circled the planet. The experts also say that our period, geologically speaking, is the twilight era for evergreens. It may be that our pines with naked seeds in imbricated cones are the link between the complicated reproductive spores of ferns and horsetails and the hard-shelled seeds that insure us our present flowering countryside.

What are the golden candles? Perhaps it is a bit of literary license, but if you will look at the white pines in spring on a sunny day as the new growth is starting, the tip ends

147

have a golden-brownish hue. The white pine is a beautiful tree, tall and graceful, submitting to the tempests of winter and standing serene again after the storm has blown out. Its flowers are small stiff catkins. It takes two years for the five- or six-inch cones to ripen. The light seeds are often carried far in the autumn winds. Two tiny seeds are encased on each scale. Gone now are the magnificent stands of "mast" pines that New England once had, but they still grow on our hillsides, along the edges of valleys, and on mountain shoulders. And every spring the golden candles are lighted again.

A third picture I enjoy in spring is the old-fashioned purple lilac. Wherever I travel, I see the purple pyramids in May. I remember the long lilac hedge on Glenrose Farm; I remember the clumps of shrubs in the village cemetery. Lilacs on Decoration Day helped us to remember the sacrifice of those who fought and died for our country. I often see lilacs along neglected upland roads beside the crumbling cellar holes that mark the homes of yesteryear. Each spring the buds break and for a few days the glowing soft color is a part of the miracle of spring. The purple lilac, like the peony, is a symbol of home and a link with those who have gone before.

When I was a lad on Glenrose Farm, I often used to go tramping through the woods in search of spruce gum.

I cannot say for certain whether black spruce or red spruce produced the better gum. The *Britannica* states that gum comes from the black species—*Picea mariana*. Schuyler Mathews says that all the spruces produce a gum but that the Red is the most abundant conifer of the White

Mountain region. "All the spruces yield the commercial spruce gum. It is collected in the winter from punctures made on the trunk in the previous spring. Spruce beer is made from a decoction of the fresh twigs of the Black and Red spruces."

There was a time when spruce gum was important commercially, and several hundreds of men went into the northeastern woods to harvest the chunks of oozed material. I have seen one estimate that 150 tons of spruce gum were harvested in Maine in the 1900 era.

I used to harvest my supply in the late winter. I always chose a pleasant cold day after a thaw so that I could walk on the crust. I had a few favorite spruce trees and I made gashes in them the previous spring so that I could readily harvest big clean chunks. I took along a good-sized screw driver attached to a long handle; this sometimes saved me the trouble of climbing into a tree.

I knocked down a couple of good big chunks and took them back to the house. It was a good idea to trim the pieces of gum before I put them away in a shoebox in the lower drawer of my bureau. I got rid of the bits of bark that clung, and trimmed off the rough edges and any soft spots. Then from time to time I'd cut off a chunk and chew it into a pleasant purplish-magenta ball. If it was first-quality gum it was chewable a considerable number of times. And I always remembered to take it out of my mouth at night and stick it to the back of my bedpost. It is not wise to try to keep spruce gum in your mouth overnight.

Later on in the spring I always made a trip to the woods to look for willow whistles. A country lad trudging a dirt road to District School was not properly equipped unless he had several whistles in his pockets, along with a jackknife, a chunk of spruce gum, cigar bands, lucky coins, a horse-blanket safety pin, and an advertisement telling how to make a quick fortune raising ginseng.

It was not a complicated task to make a whistle. When the life juice runs strong in the spring, it is easy to loosen the bark on a willow twig by steady tapping. You hold the knife by the blade and tap with the body end. After a bit of all-over tapping, the bark slides off in one piece. A V-shaped notch cut before the tapping determines the pitch, and to some degree the volume, of the note. With half a dozen whistles in his pocket, a boy had a choice of music to add to the melody of the birds.

Pussy willows make the best whistles. The easiest-sliding bark comes from shrubs along meadow brooks where ample moisture is available. In early spring the rich abundant juice lubricates the wood just inside the outer bark layer. If a boy started for school a few minutes early, he could set his lard-pail lunch bucket on a stone wall and go to the willows by the brook. Plump gold and black bumblebees worked the gray-fur blossoms for nectar and pollen. Other small bees and insects made soft music as they began the season's housekeeping. A young man with some experience hunted until he found the sizes he wanted—branches varying from the size of his little finger to the size of his thumb. Other willows could be used, but the bark of the black and the swamp willows did not tap loose so easily.

The willows are members of an ancient family. A hundred million years ago willows were growing in the

Potomac region along with poplars, elms, and sassafras. No one knows precisely the number of species of willows; some 200 species have been described, but in addition there are many natural hybrids. Wherever you go, you hear stories of willows that have grown from fishing poles or walking sticks thrust into moist soil. Conservationists use this power of the willow and plant twigs on stream banks and roadsides to hold sloping soil in place.

The White Willow is our largest common willow, but the Black in the Mississippi Valley sometimes reaches a height of a hundred feet. The pussy, or Glaucous, is most frequently found as a shrub, although in favored northern sections of the Northeast a pussy willow may attain a diameter of eight or ten inches. But come May and true spring, a country lad isn't concerned with botanical facts. He just wants several willow whistles available as he ambles along the road to school.

I always enjoyed working with the livestock on Glenrose Farm. I can still see the big barn with its dozen milking cows, half a dozen neatstock, and three or four young calves. I remember Old Jerry and Charlie, the patient plodding farm horses, and the welcoming whinny they gave me when I went out to do the afternoon chores.

Unlike most farm families, we finished the chores before supper. The common practice around here was to feed and water the stock before supper; after supper, men and boys did the milking. On a dark afternoon, I lit a kerosene lantern and went out through the ell. When we first bought the farm, the long ell connected the house with the barn; but Father felt it was a fire hazard so we took off a long section, perhaps forty feet. The original ell was one of the longest I have seen.

When I opened the sliding door to the barn, the horses whinnied and the hungry cows rattled their swinging stanchions. Buttercup, the first cow we bought, had her place at the near end of the tie-up, and she always mooed in a low voice, about A flat below low C. Here and there about the barn were oaken pegs on one of which the lantern hung while I fed the cows and horses their hay and grain, took care of the neatstock, and cleaned out the tie-up. I did various chores while the corn meal and small potatoes were cooking in the outdoor kettle for the pigs. I can hear those pigs' high-pitched squealing now as they waited for their supper.

I liked the smell in the barn—a smell compounded of horse and cow, hay, grain, leather in the harness room, and old lumber of the barn that may have been close to a century old. It is admittedly a strong pungent smell, but in a clean-kept barn the manure smell is not too powerful. When I bedded down Old Jerry and Charlie for the night with fragrant swamp grass that we cut in the low end of the meadow, there was a clean heady fragrance from the coarse grass. After I cleaned out the cows' stalls, I scattered a deep layer of sawdust under the cows and in the gutter. Father was particular about the barn and I took pride in earning my 10 cents a week for chore work. We were one of the very few families who brushed the cows' flanks and washed their udders with warm water before milking.

When I go into a barn these days, there is no friendly whinny from a farm horse; there are no rattling stanchions or low-pitched, impatient moos from a string of cows. The tractor and the mowers are lined up in geometrical precision. Tools hang on the wall. There may be a barrel of sand for ice storms, and a grindstone covered with an old bath towel. It is neat and orderly, but those machines and tools can't talk to a man.

All over northern New England the great gray ghosts of the old barns still stand, staunch and true. Windows are broken and some of the up-and-down boards are gone. Perhaps the big doors are missing, but the roof lines are still straight. A century and a half ago, it may be that a man and his sons spent a winter getting out the timbers for one of these barns. They adzed them square for certain places, and only on one side for other spots. They hauled great hemlock and pine logs to a nearby mill for boards; they hauled oak and maple for the floor planks. And when a spring and summer had passed, one fall day friends and neighbors from miles around came to the barn raising. Ahead of time, the farmer and his sons had framed the sides and ends.

It was a big event in the countryside. The womenfolk prepared a feast, and perhaps there was a hogshead of rum bought especially for the raising. And when the sides and ends were up and trunnels in place, they lifted the rafters and put up the ridgepole. Then some man, noted for his daring, walked the length of the pole and the farmer knew the hardest part was done, and the barn was properly dedicated.

I like old gray barns. They are part of the history of our country. They were built big and true and solid. Men dreamed big dreams of a new nation in a new land as they raised their barns, just as I dreamed big dreams while I did the chores in our barn.

Of all the chores in the barn, I liked tending the horses best. I enjoyed keeping Old Jerry and Charlie sleek and well groomed, but there was a time in late winter and early spring when they could shed an unconscionable number of hairs no matter how thoroughly I currycombed and brushed. There is nothing like a few hairs in your mouth and inside the collar of your shirt to teach you a certain lesson. I don't know just what that lesson is, but when Father was briefly stymied for a moral lesson when I complained about something, he always fell back on one of his favorite words—forbearance.

Nature has ordained that fur-bearing animals shed their coats, and so far as I know all of them in our North Temperate region shed in the spring. Certainly horses, cows, and dogs do. I have just looked in several books, and don't know yet whether fur-bearing animals grow extra hairs in the fall for winter protection, or whether the fur they have in the fall simply lengthens. Whatever the reason, Old Jerry and Charlie seemed to get rid of a lot of hair.

I used to tie them to a post in the barnyard and go at them with currycomb and brush. I liked to use a curry-comb that the mail-order catalog called the "New Galvanized and Oxidized Steel Currycomb." It had eight rows of steel teeth that pulled out sizable gobs of old hair. After one or two strokes I had to use a ten-penny nail to pry out the matted hair. But the important point was that you really got a load of the hair. I can still remember how Old Jerry would lean hard toward me as I was currycombing. I imagine that the steel teeth felt mighty good against his skin.

I remember too, on the Saturday mornings when I could spend time with the horses, how Old Jerry would not stand still until he had his cookie or perhaps half a doughnut. Once he had his bit of sweet, he would thoroughly enjoy the grooming. There was one time in my life, when I was about twelve, that I kept a two-quart lard pail hidden behind the grain chest. In this pail I kept an emergency store of Mother's sugar cookies, a few dough-nuts, and occasionally a chunk of gingerbread. I needed these for the horses.

After the currycombing came the brushing, and my favorite brush was the catalog's Special Quality Extra High Grade Rice Root Horse Brush. It was about ten inches long and two inches wide. It had a strong leather thumb and leather finger guards. I have wondered for years what that term "rice root" means.

Boys don't have the opportunity to currycomb a friendly farm team today. They may polish up the farm tractor occasionally, but that isn't like combing a horse that obviously enjoys having his coat groomed, and that will nuzzle a fellow's jumper pockets for a bit of cookie. Of course, you don't get horse hairs in your mouth working around a piece of machinery.

Harness oiling was a job I never looked forward to. On a rainy Saturday when I wanted to go fishing, it was almost a certain bet that Father would look at me as we finished breakfast and say, "Haydn, wouldn't this be a good day to oil the harnesses?" Now the fact that Father put his wish in question form had nothing to do with my opinion. What Father was really saying was, "Haydn, oil the harnesses today." I argued a good deal, according to my sisters, but there are arguments and arguments. One time I did not argue was when Father had a specific job in mind for me to do.

A good farmer was proud of his horses and his equipment. The first step in oiling a harness was to wash it, and that meant I had to take the harnesses apart. On Glenrose Farm there were three harnesses: two sets of work harnesses and the lightweight harness used on the Morgan roader. I got everything together in the cluttered farm shop. I built a fire in the stove and heated water. We had a couple of battered old tubs, and after I took a harness apart the leather pieces went into warm water to soak. I think I used some special soda or soap—I cannot recall exactly. But the soaking made the leather pliable and easy to clean.

There was a plank trough that ran from a sawhorse

to a tub. On this sloping trough each piece of leather was scrubbed and the water ran back into the tub. A stiff-bristled brush took off the softened dirt. The water became a whiffle darkish as the work went on, but it was good to feel the leather growing soft and to see how much better it looked when clean.

It was monotonous work, washing and scrubbing the traces, breeching body, choke straps, breast straps, nose straps, blinds, winker stays, reins, hip straps, throat latches, round side reins, breast collars, crupper, saddle strap, bellybands, and holdbacks. It took two or three changes of water to do all the harnesses. As each one was scrubbed, the pieces were put in separate piles, for Charlie and Old Jerry were slightly different in build and the harness of each horse had to fit.

Then came the oiling. You can oil leather while it is still wet, for as the moisture dries from leather, the oil will work in. I used plenty of harness oil to start and then wiped off any surplus. Last of all, there was a special harness dressing to rub into all the pieces. When the washing, oiling, and dressing were done, it was not too hard a task to assemble the harnesses and hang them back on their oak pegs. I was glad of Father's praise: "Good work, Haydn. The harnesses will go through haying." I liked his next words even better. "Why don't you go down to the meadow brook and get us a mess of trout for supper?"

I was always pretty good with the farm animals. I liked them and they seemed to like me. The horses were my favorites, but after them came the cows. There's a special satisfaction in caring for a cow, and once you get the hang of it, milking is fun too. But most fun of all is the pleasant battle of teaching a calf to drink from a pail. A baby calf is an appealing little creature with big wondering eyes, floppy ears, and wobbly slender legs. But cute as they are, they usually have minds of their own.

Father always claimed that a good cow should give milk ten months a year and go dry for two months. I remember that certain cows were recalcitrant about drying up. Other bossies seemed more than willing. In order to keep the milk supply coming, a cow should produce a calf about once a year. Anyway, Nature took its course according to schedule in most cases, and a new calf meant a fresh cow—and a big supply of milk. In the old days a two-canner was a good cow. That meant she would fill two of the wooden-stoppered eight-quart cans in which we shipped milk to the city.

Our procedure was to let the new calf have the essential mother's milk for a couple of days. Then the general practice was to teach the calf to drink skim milk from a bucket. The cream saved from the milk was used to make butter. It seemed a thrifty thing to do in an era when thrift was an important philosophy of living. It was my job to teach the calves to drink, and over a period of time I evolved a technique that was reasonably workable. Recently I watched a six-month-old baby as its mother endeavored to insert bottle nourishment between its lips. It was a happy fist-pounding little type who did not understand Emily Post's directions for high-level food consumption. As the mother patiently struggled, and the future citizen blew food in diverse directions and enthusiastically pounded his fists on anything within reach, it reminded me of my long ago struggles with a baby calf.

Basically most boys believed in straddling the young calf in the pen, placing the bucket of milk on the floor, and inserting a finger in the calf's mouth. With the other hand you forced the calf's head downward. The idea was that the finger in its mouth would make the calf believe it had hold of the spigot which produced nourishment. I don't know the multisyllable psychological term involved here, but it was a logical association of ideas. While the calf was holding on to your finger, you pushed its head down until its mouth was in the milk. Theoretically all would go well once the calf got a taste of warmed milk.

Actually it did not always work out according to plan. The calf would twist and turn and in general make life interesting. The first few times a calf drank from a bucket were likely to be lively sessions. A lad with an experimental mind learned that the best way to operate was to back the calf into a corner of the pen so that the hindquarters were more or less anchored in one position. Once you had the stern under control, it was easier to operate on the bow.

Two or three sessions like that usually taught the calf that milk in the bucket was a pleasant experience. Not before one unhappy episode, however. About the second or third session, just as I felt the calf was finally getting the idea, the gentle-eyed, appealing little creature would lift its head, look at me, and let go with a gusty blow of milk that sprayed all over my overalls. Calves, like humans, eventually learned their lessons, but there were usually some unpredictable upsets along the way.

I used to think that calves were just about the most

stubborn animals I knew, but that was before I ran into my first young steer. I can remember when a yoke of steers was an everyday sight. In the 1910–15 era, when I was both sides of a dozen years of age, one of my good friends was an elderly man who lived alone in a three- or four-room house. "Old Ben," as we called him, must have been in his eighties, but his mind at the time of which I speak was crystal clear.

He used to tell us stories of farm life and country living in the 1850 period, and one of the things he enjoyed describing was training oxen. As a boy and young man, Old Ben had worked on many farms in southern New Hampshire; he was proud of his career as an ox man. In those days of a century ago, farm life was self-sufficient to a large extent. Cash was as welcome then as now, but a general farm produced much of its own food. Farmers raised all their own meats; they smoked hams and bacon and put down barrels of salt pork. The house cellar was filled with root crops come fall. They used wood for fuel and farmers always kept a good supply of dry wood. Heavy black smoke curling from a farm chimney in midsummer was a telltale badge of lackadaisical planning.

In those days, three generations and more ago, the power on the farm was ox power. Horse power was a later development, more or less concomitant with the invention of labor-saving machinery which functioned more efficiently with faster-moving animals. For even the most ardent ox supporters will admit that steers walk slowly, and I know from personal experience that you gain very little by trying to urge steers to hurry.

Not that they can't run, especially if you have a yoke

of Ayshire or Holstein steers about two years old. One of my vivid memories is the time a pair of two-year Ayshires ran away with me. Mason Whitaker had a handsome pair of young steers. They were somewhat rangy in type and had sets of magnificent brass-tipped horns. One winter day I was in the village and dropped into Mason's place. He was just yoking up the steers to walk them up and down the long street in Hancock village. It was the heart of winter and they needed exercise. I offered to exercise them, and Mason told me to go ahead. It was a well-trained yoke, so I got on the double sled and started down the slight slope at the bottom of Norway Hill.

Just about opposite the Historical Society building, something suddenly frightened the steers. I have never known what it was, and am still puzzled about the event. It was a bright sunny cold winter afternoon, and Hancock's main street in midwinter was as quiet then as it is now. But for some inexplicable reason, the steers were badly frightened. They leaped forward; they began to run at full speed. I clung to one of the front corner posts on the sled, and we went careening down Main Street, past the two stores and two hotels, past the common, church, vestry, and Grange Hall. We tore around Norway Pond and up to the depot. A bit beyond the depot, the steers decided they had had enough and stopped of their own free will. It was a wild and fast ride, and I took a good deal of joshing the rest of the winter about my methods of ox training.

Sufficient to say that even when I was fourteen, I had already learned one of life's helpful lessons. I make it a policy when something happens that is out of my control to adapt the situation to the results. In this case, when I was chided for racing the steers on the main street, I simply said that I was planning to enter them at Oak Park Fair in Greenfield the coming fall. I figured that a yoke of oxen going at full speed around the half-mile track would be an interesting and unusual feature. Mason Whitaker's reaction? Never a word of condemnation. But I would like to know what happened in those ox brains to start the runaway.

When mowing machines, iron horse rakes, and reapers became practical tools about the middle of last century, it spelled the end of the ox-power era in American farming. Not that the change-over was accomplished in a hurry; at the beginning of the twentieth century oxen were still very common in New England. When we first moved to Hancock, there were twenty-six oxen in town. A similar situation probably obtained in most northern New England towns.

So far as my research goes, the governor of Massachusetts Bay Colony imported some cattle of the Devon breed in 1634. Those large, dark red or roan cattle came from the Devonshire district of England, a district famous in cattle circles as the place of origin of modern Milking Shorthorns. An interesting historical note is that of seventeen ships arriving in New England in the year 1630, thirteen ships came from Devon and its immediate vicinity.

There is an interesting record also that in 1634 there were some three hundred head of cattle on Mason's Patents, now the state of Maine. The U.S. Department of Agriculture Yearbook of 1863 says of these cattle,

"They were large, of powerful make, and chosen for their capacity for labor and the rigors of our climate." Large, hardy, yellow-color Danish cattle were imported to New England farms at an early date. So far as I can learn, it was the interbreeding of the big reds and roans from Devonshire and the big-framed yellow cattle of Denmark that eventually produced the famous strain of "Old Red Stock of New England."

Through the seventeenth, eighteenth, and a good share of the nineteenth centuries, oxen helped "make" New England farms. Through a full two centuries, oxen were used to plow, harrow, and harvest during the growing season. In between seasonal farming jobs, farmers and their boys built thousands of miles of stone walls with the big beasts. Rocks were hauled on stone boats and made into the walls that now remind us of patchwork stitching on the hillsides and around fields.

In the fall, after the corn was shocked and the crops under cover, good farmers liked to "make" a little land. That meant pulling stumps and clearing out rocks and perhaps plowing just before freeze-up time. "Nothing to equal a yoke of well-trained steers," a neighbor farmer used to tell me, "when it comes to plowing, stump pulling, and twitching out boulders. A well-trained pair knows what to do. They go at it slowly and exert their strength slowly. They don't get flustered and upset the way horses are likely to."

Then in the winter, back in the old days, many farmers planned to do a little lumbering. There were always calls for lumber on a farm, and furthermore there was always a market for lumber in the cities to the south.

An enterprising farmer figured on getting out a hundred dollars' worth or more. For generations it was oxen that twitched logs from the wood lot to the loading spot, then pulled the double sleds to the local sawmill and hauled the boards and timbers back to the farm.

Economically oxen fitted the picture. They lived on home-raised hay and grain. They needed no expensive harnesses; a good farmer could make the yokes. And when an ox was three, four, or five years old, it meant beef for the family's food supply, and perhaps half the carcass to sell to the General Store. Most of the changes that have taken place in the rural economy have been dictated by economic or efficiency reasons. I grew up in the twilight era of ox power, but for several years I earned some welcome cash money by training young oxen.

I think I was about ten when I began training young steers for Henry, one of our neighbors. Henry was something of a character in town because he believed in oxen instead of horses, but comments were always reasonable because Henry was a prosperous, substantial citizen who put a few hundred dollars in the savings bank each fall. You have probably noticed that comments are much less caustic about a citizen's peculiarities if he has proved he can make money. Henry paid me five cents an hour for training his young steers, and after each hour's session I made my mark on the barn door. When I had put in twenty hours, Henry would dig out his old, long-pouch-type pocketbook and give me a dollar's worth of change.

In case some of you are planning to train steers, you should know two requirements come ahead of everything else: patience and gentleness. "Never get angry at a steer,"

Henry told me. "An ox isn't very bright, but once the crittur has learned its lesson, it never forgets, and that's more than I can say for some citizens of this town."

Henry had yokes of all sizes—yokes that he made. A man who raised steers needed several sizes for animals of different ages. Henry laid his pattern on a timber of straight-grained oak; then he hewed it out as far as he dared with an adze. Next he worked carefully with a drawshave until he came to the pattern lines; finally he worked long and patiently sandpapering the wood to a smooth finish. The yokes for the full-grown steers had end irons so they would not split. Holes were bored for the bow pin; the center iron and ring were put in. It was this center iron ring to which the chain was attached that pulled the load.

The first step in training a young steer is to teach it to lead on a halter. In good weather I worked in the big barnyard. I read once that a sign of intelligence is the size of one's vocabulary, and it will give you an idea of an ox's I.Q. to say that an ox has a vocabulary of four terms: Get Up, Whoa, Gee, and Haw. In working with a yoke of steers, the handler works at the left of the nigh ox.

You may think it was monotonous work, but in reality I enjoyed it. I concentrated on two commands during the First Reader stage: Get Up and Whoa. I wish I had a dime for every time I've started and stopped with a young steer. Since I enjoy keeping records of things that others consider trivial, I wish I could tell you how many times a six-month-old steer has to be stopped and prodded to a start before the commands Whoa and Get Up become meaningful. Then eventually, and usually suddenly, the young steer gets the idea. As soon as it learned the starting and stopping commands, I began to work on Gee and Haw.

Half the battle with any animal is won if the animal knows you are its friend. Kindness and gentleness are the secrets. I trained each steer individually to the four commands, and eventually there came the day when two were yoked together. Henry knew how to match steers, and once a pair were yoked together they would be a team that always worked together.

The weight of the yoke on their necks was a new experience, and the steers didn't realize it meant the beginning of work. It was slow progress for a few sessions, but finally the team caught on that they were to start and stop together, that they went to the right with Gee and to the left with Haw. Through the weeks, at irregular intervals, the training went on. Usually I had two or three pairs to train, and come spring I taught them to pull their first loads. They were yearlings by this time and weighed perhaps six to seven hundred pounds, for Henry was a good feeder. The second summer the young steers were put out on a mountain pasture, and then the training was continued in the fall. But the knowledge the oxen had learned quickly came back. I never lost the lesson of patience that I learned either. It has stood me in good stead for years.

Of all the animals I worked with, Old Jerry was my favorite. He wasn't more than ten years old when Father bought him—a slow-plodding, faithful farm horse. The man from whom we bought him said his name was Old

Jerry—and Old Jerry he was from that day until the day when time ended for him, ten years later.

I was also ten years old the spring we bought him, and Father said, "He is yours, son. He's sort of thin now and gaunt, but he's the type that will fill out. He hasn't been fed much but poor hay this winter. On good hay and a little grain I think you will have quite a horse."

Old Jerry and I hit it off from the beginning. Each morning it was Old Jerry's whinny that welcomed me when I opened the barn door to start the morning chores. I fed him first of all. I saw to it that he had a generous measure of whole oats and a little cornmeal. Day by day, that first spring, you could see the flesh come on his ribs; you could see the hip bones cover with flesh and watch his neck fill out. Each morning, even on school days, I used the currycomb and brush to get off the old hairs; and on Saturdays I gave him a real going-over. Old Jerry became "my" horse, and if I were working around the buildings, I let him out and he followed me around. Whenever I could fool my sisters and snitch a few cookies from the kitchen, I always shared them with him.

Old Jerry and I worked together. By the time I was twelve or thirteen, I was plowing in light soil fields. Old Jerry plodded along slowly and I, with the reins around my neck, hung onto the one-horse plow. When we hit a rock, Old Jerry stopped; he knew how to take a wide swing at the end of a furrow. When we cultivated corn and beans, I just wrapped the reins around the cultivator handle. Old Jerry walked the middle of the row; he obeyed Gee and Haw perfectly.

He was a big and powerful horse, and we did much

MEMORIES OF A COUNTRY BOYHOOD

of our mowing with a one-horse mowing machine. Old
Jerry and I mowed and worked together on the horse
rake. He pulled loads of hay to the barn, and then he
pulled the hay fork that lifted great loads to the mow.
In the spring, after Father had finished the pruning in
the orchard, Old Jerry and I went along with the hayrack
and gathered up big loads of brush that we carried to a
pile in a field to be burned.

It was a sunny April afternoon that Old Jerry died.
I took care of him that morning as usual, and he nuzzled
my pocket for his cookies. His whinny was as eager as
always and his big bright eyes gave me greeting. After
the chores and his grooming we went to the sidehill
orchard to gather brush. He swung his big head around
and watched me, and when I told him to go ahead, he'd
go fifteen or twenty feet and stop. Every once in a while
I went up to him and rubbed his nose and gave him a
doughnut I had in my pocket. He munched the doughnut and then, as he had the habit, he nuzzled my shoulder,
telling me he could stand another doughnut. I scratched
him around the ears, told him not to expect too much,
and went back to work.

A minute or two later I heard a crash. Old Jerry was
down. His time was up and he lay down and went to
sleep. The April sun was as bright as ever and the blue-
birds and robins were singing. The mountains across
the valley were serene against the sky. But my friend was
gone. Old Jerry died that sunny April day. And there's
still a little blank space in my heart when I think of him.

Half a century ago, farmers, villagers, and even suburbanites kept a flock of hens. A man got up at a decent hour in the morning, say 5:00 A.M. in summer and 6:00 in the winter. While his wife prepared an honest breakfast of hot cereal, bacon and eggs, toast from homemade bread, grape jelly, and coffee plus a piece of juicy rhubarb pie left over from last night's supper, a man went out to feed and water his hens.

Of course, even in 1900, there were undoubtedly a few citizens who didn't care for hens. That is inevitable in a democracy; but the number of men who didn't like hens was a small proportion of the electorate. A man who likes hens is the first to admit that a hen is not one of the higher intellectual types of animal life. When you try to drive a hen in a straight line, she displays the same kind of perversity that often characterizes animals of the higher orders.

Hens can be very stubborn and individualistic, but they make up for their short comings in other ways. They provide broilers, roasters, and eggs. And believe it or not, hens are excellent conversationalists; they appreciate your opinions. Urban dwellers cannot be expected to know the facts, but if you talk to biddies, they inevitably respond. They listen respectfully as you enunciate opinions you would not feel free to communicate to your neighbor; you can sound off on any subject and a hen does not bristle with contrary opinions. A hen never asks embarrassing questions.

It is genuinely relaxing to sit on a box with the hens scratching near by in clean oat straw. They pause from time to time to answer in a throaty, friendly fashion. They come close to pick tentatively at your shoelaces.

Occasionally a feathered lady wants a bit of petting and you have a chance to rub her glossy feathers. Some people think a hen is a bit boastful because she sings a loud hymn of praise after laying an egg. It may be a matter of opinion, but it seems to me that an egg is quite an achievement and that a hen has every right to announce its arrival.

On Glenrose Farm it was one of my spring tasks to hunt eggs. We kept the layers shut in the pen until noon, for most hens perform their duty in the forenoon. Then at noon Father would open the hen-house door so that the birds could wander around the barnyard picking up bugs and getting the gravel they needed to furnish grinding power in their gizzards. Even as there are individualists in human society, so there are in hen society. A few of the hens hung on and waited until afternoon before laying.

When I got home from school, it was a battle between me and the late layers to discover their nests and collect their eggs. I quickly learned most of their favorite spots, and it became a routine matter to pick up the egg in each. Old Speckle chose a corner behind the plows and cultivators in the horse barn. Each day as soon as the hen-house door was opened, she headed for the horse barn and made no bones about her objective. She had a job to do, and she did it. The fact that she liked the dark corner behind the tangle of farm implements better than the nests in the house was not held against her. She was open and aboveboard in her action. Cleopatra liked the woodshed and deposited her contribution in a corner behind the heap of knotty chunks that were used in the parlor stove.

The Queen chose the icehouse; and Ophelia used a corner of the carriage shed.

But some of the contrary-minded ladies flew up to the big haymow in the barn; one always chose the far corner of the blackberry patch. One year a lady fooled us all by choosing the interior of a huge rotted apple-tree stump at the edge of the orchard. When she brought forth a dozen fluffy, bright-eyed chicks one May day, Father said, "Well son, I see Clementine has put one over on us."

I have always liked hens, and I absorbed my first inklings of the workings of the capitalistic system with a small flock of pullets. During boyhood years I earned part of my spending money from eggs and broilers. I had a flock of twenty-five or more Barred Rocks, and I liked to go into the pen on a warm sunny spring day and talk the biddies into an extra egg or two that I could sell at Fogg's General Store.

Most of our neighbors kept from 100 to 200 hens, and most of the men had the old-fashioned lamp-burning incubators. I remember the old Cypher that we eventually bought. As I recall it, you could put about 240 eggs in the machine in two trays. Twice a day the trays were taken out; twice a day the eggs were turned by hand, and you always had to keep an eye on the thermometer to see that the heat was 103 degrees. Then after the chicks hatched, I raised them under a coal-burning brooder.

Setting a hen to hatch out a nestful of eggs was a different proposition. You make up the nest carefully for the 21-day vigil. I made the nest with garden soil to hold heat, and over the soil went a layer of chaff from the haymow. Last of all, it was lined with soft hay. It should be mentioned that a broody hen can be cantankerous. Sometimes she will set for a day or two, and then her fever will subside. That is why I always tried a hen on a bunch of china eggs before giving her thirteen good eggs. A broody hen likes a dark quiet place to put in her time, and usually she comes off the nest just once a day for food and water.

One of the tasks I enjoyed was testing the eggs for fertility about the tenth day. At night I would go out with a lantern and a piece of heavy cardboard in which a hole had been cut. By holding the cardboard hole in front of the lantern flame and putting an egg in the hole, you could tell whether a chick was developing. The dark mass of the growing embryo showed plainly. I tried to set three or four broodies at a time. Then if only eight or ten eggs in each setting were fertile, I would combine eggs and set one of the broodies on another clutch. I gave the broodies whole corn for its heat-giving value, but no matter how well a hen ate she always lost weight during the period when Nature raised her body temperature so that she could hatch her chicks.

Today hens are kept in flocks of a thousand or more, in contrast to a flock of a hundred or so when I was a boy. Gigantic impersonal machines hatch out 100,000 chicks at a time in an environment where heat and humidity are carefully controlled. A modern poultry plant is run like a factory, with food moving along on endless belts and running water always available. The biddies get a scientifically balanced ration with all the essential vitamins, minerals, antibiotics, and trace elements.

And now, moving belts behind sloping egg boxes take

the eggs away. It just doesn't seem right to me. The hen doesn't even have a nicely padded nest in which to rest a few minutes before she lays. These sloping-floored nests have a wire bottom. A hen can't be comfortable on it. It adds insult to injury to have the egg roll down and onto the belt just as soon as it is manufactured. If I were a hen, I think I'd prefer things the way they used to be.

Another bird that I had a lot to do with on the farm was the crow. Now that I come to think of it, there's not much you can do with a crow except to try to get rid of him one way or another. But their behavior puzzled me when I was a lad—and it still does. Is there such a thing as a crow convention? Do crows congregate, talk and argue, and eventually elect a leader for the flock? Do crows have political parties?

The antipathy between man and crow is easy enough to understand. It was Henry Ward Beecher who said that if human beings wore feathers, very few of us would be clever enough to be crows. If you have been brought up in the country and have known crows all your life, you know that this bird is intelligent. It is said that crows can actually pronounce words so that a person can understand them. They like to gather glistening objects, although I never saw a white pebble or piece of shining metal in a crow's nest.

The late Alan Devoe wrote, "The most extraordinary rites of a flock are the 'trials' they conduct. When a crow has broken the laws of crowdom, the flock gathers in judgment, parleying sometimes for hours while the offender waits some distance away. Suddenly the discussion ceases; there is a moment of silence. Then the flock either rises in unison and leaves, or dives in a mass upon the offender, pecks out his eyes, and pummels him to death."

I have never witnessed this ruthless scene, but a few times I have seen what I called a convention. A sizable flock usually settles on a meadow or hillside. From forty to sixty birds stand around, move in and out, caw and jabber away. It almost looks as if certain birds are favorite sons, trying to round up votes. A part of the convention that always amuses and interests me is that half a dozen big fat fellows sit in a nearby tree, apparently calm and unconcerned. From time to time a bird from the ground flock flies into the tree, holds a conference, and then returns to his duties on the convention floor. It is almost human. The big boys know that the delegates must have a chance to blow off steam, so they can feel their importance.

I recall one crow convention that lasted from mid-morning until late in the afternoon. There was loud talk and milling about all day. And all day the big boys sat in a tree a short distance away. The convention was going full blast when suddenly the crows in the tree flew down to the hillside. All the noise ceased. All the movements ended. The crows on the ground simply stood still. The leaders, if they were leaders, stood in a small group to one side.

Then, almost magically, the crows began to walk slowly away—all except one big black bird in the center. In a jiffy he was a lone figure, the center of a circle. He stood there for many seconds; it may have been half a minute. Then suddenly but unhurriedly, he lifted himself into the air. Unhurriedly all the others followed. The flock

175

winged its way across the field, above the hillside orchard, and into the evergreen woodland. The convention was over; a leader had been elected.

Not many folks realize that scarecrows have nothing to do with scaring crows. It is a kindly, thoughtful gesture to erect a scarecrow in a corn field. It offers a convenient perch for the crow that is on guard while the others dig up the kernels of corn. We should all be kind to birds, and since a man cannot expect to compete on equal terms with a crow, he might as well co-operate.

A topflight scarecrow is a work of art. I spent many an hour in the cluttered farm shop putting together a scarecrow. An apprentice might be satisfied with a stake and nailed-on crossbar, but a master craftsman went at his scarecrow in a different spirit. With a combination of holes and bolts, arms and legs could be fastened at artistically satisfying angles. The crux of the matter, however, was the face cut in silhouette. It was here that the true craftsmen, fired by artistic zeal, let himself go to achieve a facial outline that resembled some well-known character in town. Caricatures are the joy of political cartoonists and scarecrow builders alike, and even a small town had one or more citizens whose profile was readily recognizable.

On a stormy day when the rain and sleet were playing tick-tack on the windows of the farm shop, it was an interesting sport to draw a profile on paper and to judge if it resembled the person you had in mind. It often took several attempts and considerable erasing before I got just the angles and curves that did the trick. Then I cut out the profile and traced around it on a piece of half-inch clear white pine. It was not too difficult to saw it out and attach it to the body.

The secret of a first-class profile was to exaggerate certain features of the citizen who was being honored. A nose, chin, forehead, or Adam's apple were excellent media for exaggeration. A solid frame with its arms and legs, plus the profile, was worth all the effort involved. Dressed for its destiny and placed near enough to the road so that all could see it, a scarecrow added interest to the landscape.

Webster defines a scarecrow as "An object, usually suggesting a human figure, set up to frighten crows." That is technically correct, and I suppose about as good as you

can expect from some one who hasn't had any first-hand experience with crows. The point is, as all countrymen know, that a scarecrow is not set up to frighten crows. It is set up to provide interest for human beings. As long as a man keeps that in mind, he won't be too disturbed when he sees a crow using the object as a convenient lookout perch.

Half a century ago, the woods on our farm resounded with the drumming of the cock partridge. On a beautiful, mellow, gold and white March day, I often walked the orchard slope behind the barn to study the fruit buds on the apple trees. I could feel the chains of winter loosen; I could hear soft monotone sounds as the land relaxed from winter's taut grip. Suddenly I heard the drumming, a reverberating, echoing message. A cock partridge was drumming his challenge.

Partridges, I am told, will drum in any month of the year, but on Glenrose Farm I recall hearing the roll calls only in March and April. Many erroneously think the drumming is caused by the wings striking the breast; some think the noise comes from the wings hitting each other above the back. Experts have proved that the drumming is produced by the concussion of air produced as the rapidly moving wings come close to the body.

The correct name for the bird is Eastern Ruffed Grouse, and of all the wild birds that I know, a cock grouse most resembles the pictures of Napoleon. I have watched a cock strut in a woodland clearing. He throws his breast out; he holds his head high; his bright beady eye has a look of imperial command. When he struts he reminds me of a miniature turkey, with tail spread fanlike, the ruff lifted around his neck, and his topknot crest standing up. It is one of the most interesting woodland wildlife scenes I know.

When we first came to Hancock, Father said we would have trouble with the birds. Our Baldwin orchard was a favorite feeding place for them. Along the north side of the orchard was a woodland—pines, hemlocks, and spruces —just the right winter environment for partridges. When the snow was deep on the ground, the grouse fed on tree buds, and they were very partial to apple buds. If they ate only the leaf buds it would not be so bad; but logically enough they prefer the fat, larger fruit buds. Year after year, the grouse took many bushels of apples from us. As soon as I could handle a shotgun, Father paid me 25 cents a bird for all I could get. Some people think that a partridge weighs three or four pounds. I have never weighed one that I recall, but my guess is that it may weigh around a pound and a half. When you dress one, there is remarkably little meat other than on the breast. Mother needed several of the breasts to make a partridge stew for the family.

In the time of cold and snow, partridges gather for the night in a clump of dense-growing spruce or hemlocks, and as a boy I knew several places on the farm where they roosted for the night. In the time of a blizzard, they will go into a bank of snow to wait out the tempest. If, perchance, the snow is moist and a hard freeze comes immediately, the frozen crust is a death trap for them.

When I am walking in the woods and a partridge explodes just a few feet away, I still start involuntarily. That sudden explosion with the loud whir of wings upsets me. One moment the woodland is peaceful and my thoughts may be far away. Then comes the sudden, shattering noise as the bird takes off. I never was much of a shot on the wing. By the time I got a hold on myself, the bird was well away. More than once I have come upon a mother partridge with a brood of tiny brown chicks. The chicks scatter and hide, and the mother puts on a great show. She flutters around as if she were hurt and usually utters cries of distress. If you stand still when this happens, the mother tries to lead you away; but if you don't follow, she will come back and put on a real vaudeville act circling around.

I still smile when I think of one of the funniest nature sights I have ever seen. I was walking to school one spring morning and stopped for a drink at a spring, a few yards in from the road. As I approached the spring, a mother partridge began to put on her act. There were eleven of the tiny chicks and they went for cover at the mother's command. The mother fluttered around and made a great to-do, and the eleven chicks stuck their heads under leaves. It happened that the eleven faced away from me. Their little rear ends were all exposed in my direction and they were almost in a line.

I am always glad to hear the kettledrums rolling in the woodland. It brings back memories and it tells me that once again the miracle of spring is coming to the countryside.

CHAPTER SIX

NO MAN can be lonely who enjoys tending a fireplace. There is something intimately companionable in the colored, leaping flames; there is understandable music in the cheerful crackling.

Some people with prosaic minds think fireplaces are utilitarian affairs; some consider a fireplace an essential accessory to a carefully contrived atmosphere of chic and style. The true keeper of the hearth knows that an open fire has nothing to do with such attitudes. A fireplace is a cherished sanctuary for a man in a world that seems to grow increasingly complex and frustrating. The lighting of the first fire in early autumn is a ritual that deepens in meaning each year as life's trail lengthens.

To satisfy those who enjoy tending a fire, certain basic requirements are fundamental. First of all, the fireplace and chimney must be correctly built, for a hearth with

181

faulty construction and a chimney with weak draft are frustrating. Time was, a century and more ago before cast-iron stoves became common, when certain men in rural regions made names for themselves as master craftsmen in constructing fireplaces that performed well.

Thoreau wrote, "Fire is the most tolerable third party," and indeed, a good friend who does not insist on talking all the time fits the environment well. But when it comes to building the fire, a man should be his own company. First of all, and contrary to the antiseptic inclinations of allegedly good housekeepers, there must be a deep bed of ashes. A spotlessly clean fireplace is as incongruous as a wedge of apple pie unaccompanied by a generous piece of cheese. I have known a goodly number of experienced and expert hearth tenders and have yet to meet one who does not cherish a generous bed of ashes.

A solid backlog of rock maple, red oak, or ash is the next essential. Then arrange a dozen or more pieces of dry pine branches for quick-burning kindling. Over the pine kindling place the smaller logs. Crinkle a few sheets of paper; tuck the paper under the kindling and light. It takes a bit of time for the hearth to get warm and for the bed of ashes to throw pleasant heat.

The best firewood, of course, is that which a man cuts and bucksaws for himself. And if you are fortunate enough to have a wood lot, you can cut with the hearth in mind a year ahead of time. White pine burns brightly and throws an intense heat with low gold and russet flames, laced with steel blue. A half-burned pine log shows glowing coals in squares with shadows that run back and forth. White maple burns steadily with reddish-tan flames which have streaks of pure gold and a blue-gray sheen near the log. There is no crackling and few sparks. The flames are often in the shape of an inverted V, reminding you of a symmetrical pointed spruce. Elm, a tough and wavy-grained wood, burns with russet flames and leaves a log with rectangularly patterned ashes.

Black cherry chuckles and talks to itself with low-pitched staccato snaps and crackles. The flames cling close to the log and paint a brilliant picture of orange, gold, and tan, resembling northern lights playing close to the horizon, with the main body of light casually moving from one spot to another. Dry spruce is the orator of the fireplace; it shouts and emphasizes its points with snappy explosions and tosses live sparks onto the rug. Gray birch, if stored under cover immediately after cutting, is good company; it burns freely and generously and has good-sized flames of orange-gold. Bits of flame often leap from the main body and change to a purple-violet hue. Occasionally the flames run horizontally for a few moments. Best of all is old hard apple wood. It burns with dependable steady assurance; the beautiful flames of gold and orange are intermittently laced by streaks of blue and gray. And as it gives itself to the consummation, a spicy fragrance fills the room.

The true keeper of the hearth is a fortunate man. He knows the secrets of the right-sized fire; he learns about various woods. And as he watches the flames leap upward, he knows that he who nurtures a fire on his hearth also nurtures dreams in his heart.

Fireplaces have had a strange history. Their popularity seems to rise and fall with the passing years. In the old days, every farmhouse in New England had a fireplace, sometimes one in every room. But with the coming of coal- and oil-burning stoves and furnaces, the fireplace faded into the background. We had two fireplaces on Glenrose Farm, one in the parlor and one right above in the bedroom Mother and Father used. In nippy weather there was always a cheerful blaze on the parlor hearth. But fashions changed and Mother had her heart set on a base heater for the parlor. We didn't blame her; you had to get pretty close to the fireplace to feel its warmth, and it was a time-consuming job to keep it clean and well stocked with wood.

It was an exciting day when the depot agent called and told us the new base heater had arrived on the morning freight from Boston. We were on a party line of some sixteen homes along the valley road, and by noon the town knew all about it.

We had a good apple crop that fall and Father paid off a chunk on the mortgage. He paid the taxes, bought a piece or two of necessary equipment, and had a little left over. In those days people had the strange idea of paying for things when they bought them.

"Rosie," Father had said one evening, "I think we can afford that new base heater you've been wanting. You make out the order and we will send for it."

The mail-order catalog gave a full page with a large illustration to the stove. Advertising writers were just as enthusiastic half a century ago as they are today. "Status seeking" may be a new term but it has a long tradition. If you have voted in a dozen presidential elections like I have, you know that a farm family hadn't

reached the social pinnacle until it possessed a fringe-top surrey, a parlor organ, and a dignified, nickel-trimmed, urn-topped parlor heater.

"The Brilliant Base Heater is the handsomest stove on the market," the catalog said. "Inexpensive enough for every home and suitable for the most wealthy. The finest the world produces. An artist's dream in design. Embodies the best features of every heater made with the defects of none. We put more trimming on the Brilliant Base Heater than is used on any other. Magnificent, large, ornamented spun brass nickel urn, the handsomest urn ever made, with full nickeled hearth plate, heavily nickelled ash doors and corner wings; stands on heavily nickelled plate frame with nickel plated legs. Handsomely finished mica doors. If you do not find you have got one of the handsomest heating stoves you ever saw, such a bargain as you never saw or heard of, such a stove as was never seen in your section, you are at liberty to return it to us and we will cheerfully refund your money."

The heater was 53 inches high to the base of the urn, weighed 375 pounds, and cost the astronomical figure of $19.30. You could buy a pretty good dry cow for that sum, but Father believed in a balanced philosophy and after all some money should be spent on the home.

The heater sat on a zinc mat against the inside wall of the living room. The wood box was beside it, and it was my job to keep that wood box filled. Every afternoon, as soon as I returned from District School and changed into farm clothes for the evening chores, I took a metal bucket and small shovel and cleaned out the ashes.

Father and I could never be certain which spring Saturday Mother would announce at breakfast, "Frank, I wish you and Haydn would move out the stove today." Stove-moving day was a regular semiannual chore, but I have never known a logical reason why that handsome heater had to be moved from the parlor in spring, stored in a back room all summer, and then rolled back again to the parlor in the fall. The more beautiful the Saturday morning, the better the day for stove moving! If we had an early spring, the stove went to its summer resting place in April; but the fourth month is tricky in this region, so usually it was about the first of May when Mother made the decision.

When she made her announcement, Father just nodded and we finished our breakfast leisurely. It was an honest meal; after the cornmeal mush, ham and fried potatoes, toast and jam, we tamped things down with a few of Mother's crisp, tangy gingersnaps. Then we were fortified for the job.

Moving the stove, per se, was not a hard task, but it was slow and careful work. The part that I remember most vividly was taking down the stovepipe. The black, lightweight-metal pipe had two or three sharp angles where the pieces were fitted together, and naturally after months of use there was plenty of soot. Mother and my sisters spread newspapers over the floor, and Father tapped gently at the joints to break the sections apart. The perversity of inanimate objects is well known, and inevitably one of the joints in that pipe gave way unexpectedly. Soot flew out. My sisters shouted instructions. Mother accepted the situation as part of the price. It was my work to carry the sections of pipe through the dining room, kitchen, back room, and out the woodshed door to the back yard where later I tapped out the soot. Then they were greased and shined and put away for the summer.

We lowered the stove from its nickel base to small, peeled, hardwood rollers about four inches in diameter. I can remember when Father made the rollers and the spot in the attic where we stored them. Once the stove was down on the rollers, the moving began. Slowly we pushed the big bulky thing ahead. As soon as the stove had moved a few inches, another roller went under the front edge. Foot by foot we gained ground, and at last it came to its summer resting place in a corner of the back room. Here Mother and my sisters went to work and shined it up. Then from somewhere came old tattered cotton blankets and one or two worn-out patchwork quilts. All summer long the stove sat there in its colorful glory, and we had the use of the living room without a stove.

At first we burned wood in the parlor heater. Then when we could afford it, we began to use hard coal in the same stove. Yes, that stove burned coal too. The mail-order catalog said, "Stove for all heating purposes. Burns soft coal, hard coal, coke, cobs, chunks of wood, knots, blocks, or anything that may be burned in any heating stove." Wood or coal, it didn't make any difference to me. The coal scuttle was just as hard to keep filled as the wood box.

No one knows how many millions of Americans have sat in the glowing radiant heat of parlor stoves. Next to an open fireplace, it is the most cheerful, comforting heating system yet devised. Around the stove on long fall and winter evenings, our family gathered in close-knit unity. Father read the farm journals and paper; Mother sat in her Boston rocker working at the never-quite-caught-up mending and darning, and answering questions on the spelling of Mississippi and the capitol of Idaho. My sisters and I did our lessons and played flinch, authors, and parchesi.

When it got late, along about eight-thirty, Father went through his regular ritual. He took a big yellow bowl and went down cellar for half a dozen of the fancy Northern Spies. He peeled, quartered, and cored the apples and passed them to us on the point of his knife. Then he packed the stove carefully with chunks of wood and adjusted the drafts. I knew there would be a bed of coals in the morning to start the fire; and I knew that when I tumbled from my bed long before dawn, grabbed my clothes and hustled downstairs, there would still be warmth in the heater to dress by.

The parlor was the place for my favorite youthful occupation—studying the mail-order catalog. After a wholesome supper we all gathered in the parlor, Mother in her rocker, Father in his Morris chair, and my sisters and I ranged around the circular parlor table. My sisters were always complaining that I took up too much room; but it wasn't me, it was the mail-order catalog.

It was impossible to conceal the catalog behind any of my schoolbooks. Therefore, with my three conscientious sisters always ready to call attention to me, I discovered it was much better to do my schoolwork first. I went hard at it, and in what my sisters believed an impossible time, I closed my books and moved the mail-order catalog into place. Sister Mildred, a year younger than I, but definitely smarter, and hence in the same grade with me, always piped up; but when I proved I had learned the lesson, Father's smile told me it was okay to go ahead with the catalog.

Twice a year we sent a list to the mail-order company. For weeks ahead, all of us struggled with our choices.

We had just a certain amount of capital; and the problem then, as now, was to mesh desires with available funds. I learned a valuable lesson when I studied the mail-order catalog. I learned to live by a fundamental law of economics—my outgo could never exceed my intake.

We had a vast selection to choose from, and the choice was not always easy. A farm lad who earned money from trapping needed certain equipment to increase his income. If he were developing an interest in photography, the purchase of a Conley Magazine Camera, four-by-five model, at $3.95 was a major matter. It had a twelve-plate capacity and all twelve plates could be loaded and carried in the box. A young man with an ear for music needed a harmonica, but the Hohmer Chromatic at $1.35 seemed pretty expensive, even though the catalog said, "With this wonderful little instrument you can play any piece of music, popular or classic, without skipping the half tones. It has a brass plate, 20 holes, 40 extra fine reeds, each reed space being covered with a leather tongue which makes for a purer and stronger tone." That price was a problem. If a boy could buy a camera for $3.95, it seemed to him that he should be able to get a harmonica for considerably less than a dollar. However, several of the boys had agreed to get harmonicas so we could play at the Friday afternoon exercises in school.

For years I craved a gold watch, but a solid-gold watch inlaid with a locomotive scene cost $8.98, so I compromised for the 67-cent "Very Good Running Boys' American Made Nickel Plated Watch." Even so, Father questioned this purchase. The description under the watch picture said, "It is stem wind and stem set, runs

191

30 hours with one winding. We guarantee it to reach destination in perfect running order. We have changed our source of supply; we buy them from a new maker."

A young man can dream, and that is what I did when I read about the Auto-Cycle. Most of us had bicycles, somewhat beat-up in appearance but a great help if we wished to get places quickly. That Auto-Cycle for $189.00 was a beauty. The catalog was specific about it. "The strongest, easiest riding, fastest and longest-lasting motor in the world." That's one thing I liked about the ad writers of half a century ago. They included a lot of territory and pulled no punches. "All carburetor trouble eliminated by the use of the famous Brown and Barlow carburetor. A handsomer, stronger, speedier, more comfortable, more trouble proof and a more easily controlled four horse power motor than has ever been offered."

I always enjoyed studying the section on books, and Father encouraged me to spend a generous amount on them. We had a good library in Hancock, but there were books I wanted—and needed—that I could use for reference. I was interested in nature study and the catalog carried a wide selection of books to satisfy my curiosity. I also enjoyed debating and recitations and I recall that I bought a book on *How to Become a Public Speaker*.

I have always felt that the 1911 Sears Roebuck catalog represented a high spot in my young life. It was a volume of 1266 pages, and there was a host of colored illustrations. A magnificent boy's bicycle was advertised for $20.85. The beautiful Economy Chief Cream Separator was $42.50. Women's hats resembled oversized, feather and flower-laden umbrellas; you could still get Beef, Iron and Wine

Tonic, "A Spring Tonic of Quality."

Looking at that catalog today, I find something prophetic about it. It was the end of one era and the beginning of another. On pages 1262 through 1265 are descriptions and illustrations of horse blankets. Page 1266, the last one in the book, has pictures of four automobiles and this question, "Can I afford an automobile?" The reader is urged to send for the Automobile Catalog, describing "The safe, durable, economical, easy to operate Sears, the machine that does the work of a horse and buggy, does it better, faster, cheaper."

But as a boy, I was more interested in the horse blankets. It was always a big event when Father said, "Haydn, get out the catalog and let's see what there is in horse blankets. We need two new ones." Men were judged in those days by their horses and equipment. Good farmers kept their horses well groomed and the harnesses cleaned and well oiled; the wagons were painted, and in particular a man wanted a clean colorful blanket to toss over his horse when he drove up to the hitching rail before Fogg's General Store.

I liked to read the names of the blankets and the descriptions in the catalog. Those ad writers really knew how to handle words. I had my choice of a Redbird Fancy, Hudson Plaid, Most Royal, Apache Square, Cherokee Prince, Jersey Lily, Arapahoe Fancy, Belvedere Striped, Lulu Fancy, Rose-A-Lee, Blackhawk, Hollydale, St. Lawrence Special, Rockaway Fancy, Brighton Extra, and Great Eastern Fawn. My sisters made pointed comments about my ability to choose colors. The girls were filled with art with a capital A and could paint petunias, roses, and violets on lamp shades as proof of their artistic discernment.

But Father usually let me have my choice. We bought two similar blankets to use on the horses when we went to the village for a load of grain. I chose Jersey Lily. "This blanket is less than one half the price of an all-wool blanket, but you get good wearing quality and a blanket that answers all practical purposes. Wine-colored body with rich deep heading of old gold, blue, lemon, black and white with body stripes of the same colors. Size 80 by 84 inches. Weight about six pounds. Price $2.30."

It was a lot of money, $4.60 for two blankets. But the blankets had emphatic color and real character. When you mix wine color with gold, blue, lime, black, and white, you have something that satisfies. As I blanketed Old Jerry and Charlie at the hitching rail, I knew the eyes of villagers and farmers were watching. Men didn't say anything as I went into the store to visit a bit around the stove before loading up, but I knew they approved. If a man or boy took good care of his team, it was evidence of good citizenship and meant a young fellow was developing the way he should.

As a nation we have produced some notable literature, and the mail-order catalog heads the list. Not far beneath it, however, is the seed catalog. Now you may think that seed catalogs are just for the womenfolk, but I know many a man who enjoys thumbing through them and dreaming about a summer garden. As a matter of fact, I'm one of them. There are, of course, certain individuals including many wives, who smile a skeptical smile as they watch gardening-minded men pore over the colorful catalogs.

Wives, who are inclined to be realists, call the publications "dream books."

Men who garden know that the most enjoyable gardening you can do is in a comfortable Morris chair before the open oven of a wood-burning kitchen stove. There are admittedly certain drawbacks to spring and summer gardening. One has to spade, rake, spread lime and fertilizer. Even before the crop and flower seeds pop through the soil, the weeds get a good start. However, on a winter's evening while the wind is whimpering in the chimney and the red line in the thermometer drops close to the zero mark, a man can cultivate his garden of dreams and reap a rich harvest.

The English were probably the first to publish lists of seeds and plants for sale. In the U.S. Department of Agriculture collection, the earliest American list was published by William Prince and Son, Flushing, Long Island, in 1791. The first catalog, in terms of what we today consider a catalog, was published by Bernard McMahon, an up-and-coming Philadelphia Irishman, in 1796. He established an export-import business in seeds. An early catalog published by a Scot, Grant Thorburn, had a hundred pages and offered twenty-four varieties of green peas.

It is estimated we now have some 30 million home gardens and that about 100 million seed and nursery catalogs go into the mail each year. Of course, as a man pores over the books, certain thoughts come to his mind. The beautiful catalog gardens show geometrically perfect spacings; each plant represented is a magnificent specimen of its kind. The soil is perfect texture and a weed never

195

rears its ugly head. Futhermore, apparently no artist or photographer ever runs into witch grass.

Father and I used to do our share of browsing through the seed catalog. With Mother and my sisters right behind us, it took time and study before the list was made out. We had to ponder the different varieties and study the adjectives used by the uninhibited advertising writers. I could understand all the glowing words heaped on sweet corn, muskmelons, strawberries, and cucumbers, but I never could figure out what you could say about summer squash. Finally the list was complete, and Mother and Father sat back dreaming of bright flowers and delicious vegetables growing in the summer sun. As for me, I was thinking about all the planting, weeding, and picking that was in store for me.

We had a handsome, ornate parlor organ with an upholstered stool standing against the west wall of our living room. It had been an epochal day on Glenrose Farm when Father said, "Rosie, I guess we can afford that organ you have been wanting for so long."

In those days folks always put necessities ahead of luxuries, and a solid citizen did not buy an organ or a fancy sleigh until he had such things as good stoves in kitchen and living room, good milk cows, and adequate farm equipment. By 1912 or so the tide had begun to turn on our farm. The apple orchard was coming back into production; we had a few good milkers and made milk for the Boston market. The upland field and the thirty-acre meadow were producing big hay crops. It wasn't a question of food. We had ample food that we raised ourselves.

The problem in those days was cash money. If we had a big apple crop and the crop was short in other fruit-growing areas, we received a good price for a barrel of apples. Conversely, if the nation had a huge crop, the price was low. I can remember years when the price was only a dollar a barrel and an orchardist was lucky to break even. But this particular year the price was high, around three dollars a barrel. We had a big crop and Father bought all the necessities and still felt we could afford the organ.

The Imperial Grand Organ was a magnificent thing—although at $50.95 it represented the price of a good, second-calf milker. It was a handsome piece of workmanship, with plenty of scrollwork and intricate carving. The catalog was enthusiastic. It said, "Finished Golden. It is an instrument so handsome it will grace the home of the wealthy, and at the same time is so low in price as to be within the reach of all. It is 86 inches high, 46 wide, and 24 deep. Shipping weight about 400 pounds."

Musically the large instrument had plenty of range and power. There were five octaves and four sets of reeds. There were seventeen white-faced stops; and sometimes now in the dark hours when I am trying to get to sleep, I go over the list that I memorized about half a century ago. The stops were: diapason, principal, dulciana, melodia, celeste, cremona, bass coupler, treble coupler, diapason forte, principal forte, vox humane, viola, flute, bourdon, clarinet, cornet, and cornet echo. The catalog described the tone of the Imperial Grand with definite authority: "In this respect our organs are distinct from all other organs. The tone is most exquisite, full, round,

197

resonant and susceptible to the most delicate variation. In the hands of a skilled organist, this instrument is capable of producing the most charming music."

On the more down-to-earth side, the catalog stated, "The instrument is practically dust and mouse proof and especially fitted to withstand climatic changes." The stool, plush covered, was free. But the catalog said it generally sold for $2.50. There was also a free book of instructions and a written guarantee for twenty-five years.

I would like to have an evening again with Mother at the organ and the family and neighbors gathered around to sing the old songs. It wasn't a group of trained voices, but there were rich and full voices, and in those days we all loved to sing. Some of the men had deep, resonant bass voices; there were good altos and clear, true sopranos. We instinctively responded to Mother's playing —loud or soft, fast or slow. We sang the old family songs and southern songs. We had lively, toe-tapping tunes— "Solomon Levi," "The Bulldog on the Bank," "There Is A Tavern in the Town." We sang the beloved and familiar hymns, and we usually ended with that wonderfully melodious, harmonizing "God Be With You Till We Meet Again." I can hear that harmony now—strong clear voices that gathered power as they climbed to the climax of the song that has meant much to many.

And then when the evening was done and the hot cocoa and cookies eaten, the neighbors climbed into the sleighs and pungs, and we listened to the music of the bells as the snow crunched under the runners and the twinkling stars looked down to the glowing lanterns on a peaceful country road.

MEMORIES OF A COUNTRY BOYHOOD

We didn't have such cultural advantages as radio and television in those days. We did have Lyceum Courses in the winter with magicians, Swiss bell ringers, and male quartets. Once or twice a year the traveling dog show came to town. But by and large, farm families created their own evening's entertainment with the help of various card games or the stereoscope. Mother favored the educational stereoscopic slides, Father and I liked the comedies. Each spring and fall, finances permitting, a few more sets were ordered from the mail-order catalog. Mother and my sisters were particularly fond of "Around the World in 80 Minutes," "The Pan-American Exposition," "The Wonders of America," "Across the Continent," "Lights and Shadows of New York," "Where the Sweet Magnolias Bloom," "Pilgrims' Progress," "Uncle Tom's Cabin," "In and Around Yosemite Valley," "Ramble About London," "Niagara Falls," "Chicago World's Fair," and "A Summer's Trip Through Europe."

I enjoyed those sets too. I know that human beings learn much, and easily, by looking at pictures. But Father and I liked to finish off a session of culture with a bit of dessert. It is the same principle that governs our eating habits. After some meat and potatoes, it does something pleasant to our systems to top off with a piece of pie or a dish of pudding.

The comic slides were prepared by persons with a real funny bone. I liked to read the titles: "Babies on Our Block," "Hung Up to Dry," "Finding a Man," "The Boatman Rattled," "The Leaky Bath Tub," "What Is Home Without a Mother-in-law," "The Horrid Mouse," "Warm Meals at All Hours," "The Housemaid's Hard

199

NEW ENGLAND FLAVOR

Luck," "A Tight Squeeze," "Taking Toll in Rural Districts," "Eavesdropping," "Wonder If It's Loaded—It *Was* Loaded," "Did You Say Watermelon and One Stick of Gum for Two?" The catalog said, "Our slides are taken from actual models who have studied the humorous pose artistically and with a full appreciation of the comic side of life."

Come summertime, with the nickel-plated parlor heater stored in the back room, we abandoned the parlor and sat out on the front porch. Mother and Father settled down in their wicker rockers, while two or three of my sisters fooled around on the squeaking porch swing. I was usually to be found on the front steps with my chin in my hands, thinking whatever boys think about on balmy New England evenings. Or maybe I was lying in the hammock strung between the two stately elms on our front lawn. If Mother had to go in the house for a few minutes, I often took a turn in her rocker.

I still remember that rocker. The seat and back were woven of bumpy wicker and painted green. It wasn't new, but it was as good as new and it made a pleasant rustling sound as I rocked back and forth. Father would talk about what we had to do tomorrow in a low quiet voice. From the barn you could hear an occasional noise as the animals settled down for the night. When the light began to fail, my sisters wished on the first star they saw and I took the cap off a glass jar and got ready to catch a few fireflies before I had to go to bed.

What we need these days is more front porches and more wicker rocking chairs. If a man wants to sit in one of these modern contraptions that locate his bulk a few inches from the floor and elevate his feet above the eye line, that is his constitutional privilege. But it's not for me. You can purchase a chair with various levers, buttons, switches, gears, and supersonic devices that will roll, toss, jiggle, and vibrate you. You can sit and have your back massaged, your feet tingled, and your weight decreased. But I'll take a rocking chair every time. I still cherish the old-fashioned idea that chairs were meant to rest in. And of all the types of sitting equipment evolved to date, nothing equals a good rocker.

A rocking chair is always ready and always dependable. It builds no psychological tensions and engenders no frustrations. If you have a collapsible lawn chair with its complicated angles, intricate design, and ornery actions, you're likely to lose your mental equilibrium just trying to set it up. If the cantankerous contraption folds in various unpredictable directions and pinches your fingers, you might better leave it alone. You don't face a mental hazard with a rocking chair. It is always inviting, and as you start rocking slowly back and forth, everything seems right with the world.

Naturally you want a rocking chair that fits your contours. You should have one with broad arms. A man should choose his rocker as carefully as he chooses his axe or hoe. It is a matter of private judgment and, as is wholesome in a democracy, men should disagree. Some rocking chairs under a given weight will creep forward and a man has to rise periodically, put his chair back, and start over. That is not restful. But if a man will try out a few chairs, he will eventually find one that fits, feels right, and does not creep insidiously forward.

According to legend, the first rocking chair was invented by a Cape Codder in the middle 1600's. An invalid lady in the Plymouth colony was confined to a straight hard chair during her sitting-up hours. An inventive-minded pioneer conceived the idea of a chair based on the principle of a rocking cradle. He experimented with his revolutionary idea and eventually formed two strips of wood to a curve which permitted a chair to move back and forth. As others tried the idea, the principle became widely accepted, and over the years the rocking chair became a standard piece of furniture.

The golden era of the wicker rocker was from 1890 to 1910 when summer hotels, boarding houses, village inns, and home porches had a generous supply of the comfort generators. Porches of village stores had battered old rockers where men could sit while waiting for the mail to be sorted. In comfortable chairs they would discuss the new schoolteacher, the abominable condition of the roads, and national politics. Beginning about 1910 when men started rushing through life behind steering wheels instead of traveling leisurely behind dashboards, store porches and wicker rockers went into a debilitating decline. In recent years the amazing increase of self-service supermarkets wrote a temporary finis to the pleasant custom of yesteryear. Store porches disappeared along with wicker rockers.

Now we should all unite in a campaign to reinstate rockers. A farm kitchen ought to have a comfortable old rocker where a man can sit for a few minutes while supper is being prepared and enjoy the aroma of the gravy and fried potatoes and the fragrance of the perking coffee. The farm shop should have a decrepit rocker near the rusty old stove. On stormy cold-weather days a man can enjoy the comfortable warmth as he rocks slowly back and forth and goes over the farm journals and studies the mail-order catalogs.

Businessmen are missing a bet by not providing rocking chairs on the porches of their establishments. The motel business is flourishing, but it would flourish even more if the management provided rocking chairs instead of hard-bottomed metal chairs. In the halcyon era of resort hotels, porches were lined with wicker rockers and the line-up of rocking citizens was proof that an enjoyable vacation was available.

Supermarkets should take the lead in this matter. They have shown imagination and perception in many areas. A good market today has music, baby sitters, swimming pools, banking service, flowers, playground, flower gardens, merry-go-rounds, and rodeos. They display a thousand and one items to foster impulse buying. But they have missed the best bet of all. If a store would arrange for a cool shaded porch in summer and a warm porch in winter, a man could locate himself in a good rocking chair while his wife prowled up and down the aisles and bought many more items than were listed on the back of an old enve-lope. A man could sit and smoke his pipe, argue with his friends and neighbors about baseball, and settle affairs of the world.

An old-fashioned cloth hammock comes next on my list of modern necessities. There are some men of judgment who will argue for a barrel-stave hammock, and indeed, a homemade affair can be a welcome addition to the farm's furniture. A correctly made barrel-stave hammock, well padded with some old patchwork quilts and two or three horse blankets, is not a bad resting place.

But it is a cloth hammock which fits the curves and angles of a man's anatomy. On July 15, 1886, *The Cultivator and Country Gentleman* had this to say: "Without question, a hammock is one of the greatest luxuries a farmer's family can enjoy. It gives rest, fresh air and comfort to the tired hay maker, the overheated housewife and the children. Every member of the household appreciates its comfortable luxury. Hung in the shade of trees, it is one of the most comfortable resorts on the farm. Very few yards in the country, but now have one or more of these luxurious articles swinging from their porches or shade trees."

We had a Damask Weave Hammock in our front yard on Glenrose Farm. Here is what the mail-order catalog had to say about it: "This is the most beautiful hammock ever placed on the market. Made in figured fancy weaves, damask pattern, full fancy fluted valance, with fringe and scroll pattern. There is a fancy tufted pillow and strong spreader bar. Size of bed, 40 by 80 inches. This is a large size hammock, strong, durable and very showy."

That's what I want—a very showy, strong, and durable hammock. A man in a horizontal position, with a newspaper over his face to shut out the light, can relax, doze, ponder, and plan.

CHAPTER SEVEN

THE sound of bells always takes me back to my boyhood. There seemed to be a bell for everything, and every bell had a special sound and a special meaning. I remember how the teacher used to come to the door of the District School and ring the wooden-handled bell when recess or nooning was over. If you were playing cops and robbers in the woods behind the one-room school, the notes of that bell sounded insistent and arbitrary. Teacher stood smiling in the sunshine of a blue and gold autumn day while a dozen or so youngsters slowly came toward the granite doorsteps and lined up in the traditional two-file formation—boys on one side, girls on the other. Sometimes Teacher permitted a pupil to ring the call to classes, and we could always tell. Teacher rang with a steady rhythmic motion, but a boy or girl always tried to get the maximum noise and rang too fast to achieve clear individual notes.

NEW ENGLAND FLAVOR

The most common bells in the country when I was a boy were the cowbells. A farmer did not use bells on all his cows, just on the leader—and sometimes on an individualist who liked to poke off by herself. A herd always had an acknowledged leader. The pecking order of a flock of hens is often duplicated in a herd. One cow establishes herself as boss of all; then successively there are cows who dominate all except those in the echelons above. Even as in human society, there is always one meek, fearful creature who is at the bottom of the list.

Father was particular about cowbells and would have nothing to do with sheet-metal bells made from a single piece folded and then riveted together. That type of bell gave a clanging, metallic note. He preferred the solid, melodious, brass cowbell. For several years Buttercup was the leader of our herd and she wore a sweet-toned brass bell that had good carrying qualities. In fly time, when the cows went into the dense hemlock swamp so that branches of the trees would help keep flies off, I often had to listen for minutes before I heard the notes of the bell.

I remember one cow that gave me a lot of trouble. Her name was Millie, and from her girlhood days we knew we had a problem child. But her mother and grandmother produced splendid milk with a high fat content, so Father kept Millie. She stayed by herself; she acted superior. When she freshened for the first time, she wouldn't accept her calf; in the pasture she wandered off by herself. She was an individualist and is the only cow that ever kicked me sufficiently hard to toss me across the walk behind the gutter and against the side of the barn. We gave Millie a large bell with a sharp-brittle tone. Many times, with all the other cows waiting at the bars, I had to take a turn around the pasture to locate her. I can still hear that bell tone—penetrating, higher pitched than most bells—about C sharp, for a guess.

You may not remember, but there were bells for turkeys too. Many turkey flocks had half a dozen handsome, strutting toms with bells around their necks. It was fairly common practice to keep a flock of turkeys in a pen until boys and girls reached home from school. Then the turkeys were let out to wander over fields, meadows, and orchards until dark, with boy or girl following. A turkey bell was one and three fourths inches in diameter and weighed three ounces. A metal strap held the bell on the turkey's neck. "Enables the flock to be easily located and makes the foxes shy," the mail-order catalog said.

The church bell had a distinctive, important sound. It called folks to services on Sunday morning and Sunday evening, and for Wednesday evening prayer meeting. On the night before the Fourth of July, at exactly midnight, certain youths felt it their duty to ring the bell for an hour or so, and a thoughtful church sexton saw to it that the key was available without the glass of the little box being broken.

In Hancock, the church bell was also used to give the fire alarm. In the event of a fire in the village or on an outlying farm, as soon as the alarm was telephoned to Mabel at Central, she called the store or hotel and someone raced to the church, broke the glass of the little box, took the key, opened the meetinghouse door, and soon the huge bell in the steeple was clanging out the alarm. Meanwhile Mabel gave the long ring on all lines and kept re-

peating the location of the fire. You could hear the Model
T's and four-cylinder Buicks start up all over the countryside.

That same bell in the meetinghouse tolled the hours of
my youth—hours of work and play, hours of schooling,
hours of nature study in the fields and on the hillsides. On
Glenrose Farm we were a mile and a quarter from the village, but when the atmosphere was right and the wind
favorable, the notes would float down the valley and into
my room beneath the eaves.

Many citizens prided themselves on their farm bells.
Men and boys working in the fields, or perhaps in a wood
lot not too far from the farmstead, kept an ear cocked as
the sun climbed toward high noon. When the bell began
ringing, menfolk knew it was time to head for the house
and dinner. I could tell by the ringing which of my sisters
was pulling the rope, for no two persons ring a bell the
same way. Occasionally Mother had to do the ringing and
then the bell had a hurry-up sound to it. She had no time
to waste! The roast was readying in the oven, the vegetables
were done, and she wanted to keep her eye on the apple
pie with its crust just turning to a golden brown. When
we heard her ringing, Father would smile and say, "I guess
Mother wants us to come right away."

Most of the farm bells I have known were of the type
that could be fastened to a cedar or tamarack post. You
could set either of these woods in the ground and know
they would last for years, as contrasted with woods like
birch or poplar that rotted quickly. If times were good and
crops generous, a farmer might spend $2.35 for the hun-
dred-crystalline metal farm bell that had four legs and

sat on a small platform on the shed roof. A metal frame that resembled half an ox yoke held the bell; a rope was attached to the bell and hung down just over the edge of the roof. You stood on the ground close to the shed and pulled the rope, and the bell swung back and forth in its frame.

It was an exciting day when our farm bell arrived from the mail-order company. It came to the depot in a heavy wooden box. The catalog said, "Order this high grade bell and if you don't find it perfectly satisfactory, and better than anything you can get at anything near the price, return it at our expense and we will return your money. This bell is well finished, is extra fine toned, and can be heard farther than any copper or tin bell of five times the cost, and far more durable. At our $2.35 price, the bell is complete with all mountings. Diameter at mouth 19 inches. Weight, 96 pounds." I could hardly wait until Father installed it on the shed roof.

On clear cold days in fall and winter, on sunny days in spring and summer, there was music through the countryside at noon when the farm bells along the road and across the valley pealed their notes at noon. The clear musical tones were always crisper and more distinct in good weather, but it was on a cloudy quiet day just before a storm that the notes seemed sweetest and carried the farthest. On such a high-humidity, low-barometer day, you could hear bells that you did not hear in good weather.

The first thing I learned about our farm bell was that you never rang it for fun. It was meant to serve a definite purpose. Each family had a code for calling individual members to the house. There was one code—four tolling

209

notes repeated four times with a minute or two between each set—that meant company had come. It might be a dooryard visit for pleasure, or it might be that the cattle buyer had come to talk business. My sisters and I each had a code in the event that Father or Mother wanted one of us for an errand. Once in a long while wild clanging notes rang out, and hearts beat faster as men and boys raced for home. This was the emergency call—fire or accident at home or a neighbor's. And in the country everyone responded to a call for help.

Speaking of bells, I must not forget to mention the telephone. We had a big telephone box on the kitchen wall at the farm; you stood up and talked to it like a man. And if you happened to be a boy, you could adjust the long neck of the mouthpiece to suit your own individual needs. I remember the way Father used to begin his telephone calls. He stepped up to the box, cranked out a long determined ring, and when the operator answered he said, "That you, Mabel?" Then he'd likely say, "If Bert Adams is home, I'd talk with him a minute."

Father never gave his name. He didn't need to, for Mabel knew every voice in town. She also knew whether Bert Adams was home, or whether he had gone over to Center Junction, and if so, about what time he would be home. Central knew everything that was going on. Mabel was the town's focal point of information and she was allowed to tell you the news. At exactly high noon, she gave one long ring and everyone in town listened while she read the weather report from the daily paper and perhaps gave a headline or two. Those were the days of rural free delivery by horse and buggy, and half the town didn't get the mail and papers until well into the afternoon. We all knew Mabel would ring at exactly twelve and so no one used the telephone for a minute or two before twelve until after she called.

Of course there were complications on party lines with a dozen to twenty subscribers; but if you knew that what you said would be heard by many ears, you governed yourself accordingly. It was always interesting when I called Eddie, my boy friend a mile up the road. "Hi, Eddie," I said and then heard the receivers click back on the two-pronged hooks all along the line. The conversation of a couple of twelve-year-olders wasn't very interesting.

Small town life was simple, flavorful, and compact in those days. The party line was the lifeline that bound us together. When one very long ring came, other than high noon, we knew there was an emergency. If it was a fire, the men got started even before the church bell began to ring. In the dead of night when the telephone rang, it was not only a signal of trouble but a call to the neighbors along the road; and within minutes help was on the way to a neighbor in need.

Just once more I'd like to step up to that plain brown box between the kitchen windows, turn the crank, and hear Mabel say, "Number please?" Then I'd ask her how she was and if she knew whether Eddie had gone to Peterborough with his father. Mabel would tell me, and then ask me to tell Mother that Mrs. Kent was going to call her as soon as she finished baking a three-layer chocolate cake for the Ladies' Sewing Circle dinner. That was telephone service.

Uncle Charlie the Tin Peddler was second only to Mabel when it came to keeping us abreast of the local news. The annual visit of Uncle Charlie with his department store on wheels was a highlight of the year to many farm families on peaceful New Hampshire roads. He usually came to Glenrose Farm late in the afternoon, and it was an exciting moment for my sisters and me when we saw his sleek chunky horses appear down the road pulling a rig painted in bright red, blue, and yellow. The whole family gathered to greet him, for Uncle Charlie was an institution. Everyone knew him and trusted him; he brought news from friends and relations in other towns, and his cart held a wonderful display of goods.

The cart was what fascinated me. It was a big boxlike affair with the driver's seat high at the front. Along the outside were two layers of doors—the top doors opened upward and the lower doors opened downward to form a broad shelf. On the shelves were blankets and sheets, dishes, pots, pans, cutlery, tinware, lanterns, and lamps. When the rear door was opened, you could see shelves along each side of the interior, stacked with percales and ginghams, rolls of beautifully colored silks, and various kinds of laces. There were many rolls of colored ribbons, tin tubs, copper teakettles, brooms, and baskets.

Uncle Charlie spent the night with us, and after the first greetings I unhitched his plump horses, took them to the barn, rubbed them down, watered them, and gave them feed. Uncle Charlie always went to the small room in the north end of the attic, washed, and got ready for supper and the evening. I knew that he would give me something for taking care of the team, and for many years I carried a wonderful pocketknife that was my reward one year.

It was the evening program that I remember best. While supper was going on the table, Uncle Charlie answered questions and gave us news; and Mother gave him messages to carry to friends in Harrisville and Stoddard. It didn't take my sisters long to redd up the kitchen while Uncle Charlie told us stories of Armenia and his boyhood. Years later Father told me that Uncle Charlie's family had been massacred in Turkish wars but that he had escaped and eventually had reached this country. His father, mother, brother, and sisters had all been killed. I remember now the haunting sadness in his eyes.

But we children never suspected tragedy, for he was jolly and voluble, full of jokes and fun. We knew the evening ritual. From one of his pockets he brought out a big bag of hard sugar candies. Then he brought in some of the things from his cart: bolts of cloth, silk, ribbon, and laces, and Mother and the girls had a pleasant, exciting time deciding what to buy.

I know now that Uncle Charlie was a supersalesman. He had what I believe is called today the "soft" sell. He never praised his material, never put on pressure. But he unrolled those bolts of silk, percale, and gingham and let the colors and patterns talk for themselves. He spread out laces and ribbons and buttons. It may be that the soft golden light of the brass-bowled kerosene lamp hanging above the big table deepened the colors; perhaps the dyes were softer—I do not know. But I can see those soft glowing colors today.

Eventually Mother and my sisters decided what they would buy. Usually Mother also wanted a dish or two and

213

perhaps a knife or fork. Then Mother brought out the rag bag that held scraps of linen and woolens and Uncle Charlie allowed so much per pound on her other purchases. The rag bag was a cornmeal grain bag that had been washed, and each year it seemed to fill up. I don't know how, when it seemed to me that we always wore out our clothes.

That was the business end of the evening. Then we settled down for the other side. Uncle Charlie brought in his beloved violin and for perhaps an hour he played to us—gay rollicking tunes and sad plaintive melodies. No one talked; we sat there in the big kitchen and listened and felt our hearts follow the man's mood.

In the morning we helped Uncle Charlie hitch his team to the big colorful cart. He checked all the doors and then opened one. From the shelf inside he took four bags of candy in striped red and green bags. With a smile he gave one to each of us children. Then he opened another door and took out something for Mother—a strip of lace or perhaps a small colored dish. He smiled at each of us, shook hands with Father, climbed up to his seat, and started for the next farm. A man without a country, a lonely man but a kindly one.

A train whistle is one of the most exciting sounds I know. It has been many years since a train chugged into the Hancock depot, sounding a shrill blast on its steam whistle. But when I was a boy it was the highlight of the week if I could be there to welcome old 57 on its run from Boston to Keene.

The morning train came down from Keene and reached

Hancock about seven o'clock. From all over town the milk jugs had been gathered by the "milk teams" and brought to the depot. Most of the milk was carried by men who made the daily collecting a part of their work. But there were always a few individuals who did not want to pay the exorbitant price of five cents a jug to have the milk carried: they brought in their own milk.

When the afternoon train was due, men and boys gathered in the small gray depot with its tall, potbellied, cast-iron stove. I remember the long metal stovepipe that made several turns before it went into the chimney. I remember the cluttered ticket office in the corner and the mysterious clacking telegraph key on the shelf in back of the window.

215

On the outside of the corner cubby office were posters with pictures of train robbers—desperadoes for whom $500 was offered, if you got them arrested and convicted. Many a lad in a country town has studied the pictures of these wicked men and planned how he would use $500 if he caught the criminal hiding in his barn.

Then all of a sudden, from far down the line, we heard a faint whistle—a thin high-pitched call as the train left Elmwood Junction. An old-timer would pull out his big round silver watch on a leather thong, study it carefully for a bit, and then announce, "She's about seven minutes late, but Bill can make it up on the run down through Marlborough."

A few minutes later we heard the whistle at Wilder's Crossing—a scant mile away—a louder, more insistent "whoo-whoo-who-who," two longs and two shorts that carried far back among the hills when the wind was right. Then we heard the train coming across the trestle over the end of Norway Pond. As it pulled around the corner and into the station, there was the loud hissing of escaping steam, the wild clanging of the engine bell, and the clatter of the cars as they bumped to a stop.

The heavy four-wheeled depot cart with its long iron handle was ready to be pulled beside the baggage car. The baggage man threw out the milk cans, egg crates, hen crates, and wooden boxes and kegs for the General Store. Shouts were exchanged back and forth. When everything was ready to go again, the conductor gave the signal; the engineer opened his steam valve. There were quick, ear-thumping, staccato blasts of steam. Sometimes the wheels spun a few times before taking hold. The bell clanged and

216

the cars rattled as the train got under way and headed west. If I thought about it beforehand, I sometimes put a penny on the rail, or an eight-penny nail or even a big pickerel fish hook. The weight of the train fashioned fantastic shapes and designs out of small metal objects. When the train had disappeared around the bend and everything was quiet again, I went to look for the bit of metal to add it to the other treasures in my pockets.

Today the branch lines are almost gone. The squat little depots that sat through long years beside the tracks have been sold or torn down. In some regions the rails have been salvaged and sold for scrap. The rails that are left are over-grown with weeds and covered with rust—lines of brown that cross the fields and follow the valleys, circle the hills or push through cuts made when railroading was in its heyday.

Train whistles are a thing of the past too. That long lonesome sound was music to a man's ears. The raucous blast of a Diesel engine is no substitute. Almost anything is better than that dismal bleating. I sympathize with the problems of the railroads; it is inevitable in our type of economy that many of the branch lines and smaller depots have gone the way of fire horses, oil street lamps, and buffalo robes. But there is no reason why the sweet-sad song of the train whistle must pass into history just because Diesels have replaced the old steam locomotives. I'm not an inventor but seems as though somebody could develop a whistle operated by compressed air that would sound like the old-time whistle.

I want a train whistle that the engineer can handle with his own individual finesse. I want a whistle that floats across

217

the countryside on spring and summer evenings as the Night Flyer rushes through the valley like a jeweled snake. It is a lonesome sound perhaps, but a steam whistle always strikes a responsive chord. When I heard that sound as a boy, I resolved that some day I would be on a train, riding away to life's adventures.

Saturday evening was a big event in the country. Father planned to do the chores early, and with the exception of an occasional day in haying we ate supper early, got ready, and headed for Fogg's General Store for the weekly trading session. Saturday was also bath night, and the routine was carefully planned. After supper Father took his bath in the downstairs bedroom, and climbed into his second-best suit while my three sisters did the dishes and tidied up the kitchen. Mother put pans and kettles of water to heat on top of the kitchen range. The stove had a big tank at the rear, but we needed the extra warm water for baths when we returned home from the village.

There has been a deal of attention given human bathing over the centuries. In ancient days, men went at it seriously. According to the *Britannica,* "The word bath is used for the process of immersing the body in some medium other than atmospheric air, for the purpose of cleanliness, or as a cure." Back in the days of the glory that was Greece and the grandeur that was Rome, bathing was considered an important pastime. There are pictures on old Grecian vases that show they used showers. Some citizens disagree mildly on the advantages of tub versus shower. I claim you can't get clean in a tub; you scrub off the dirt and oils, and then scrub 'em in again. In a shower, you wash the dirt off and it stays off. But I am not opposed to bathtubs, mind you, and in cold weather a good soak in hot water before I go to bed is a pleasant way of relaxing.

Benjamin Franklin brought the first bathtub to this country; it was made of copper and resembled a huge shoe with a grate on the heel to keep the water warm. On Glen-rose Farm we used a round tin tub. After we came back from a Saturday evening in the village, Father and I sat in the living room while Mother put the three girls through the wet-cleaning process in the kitchen. Then when the girls had gone to bed Mother called me, and always said the same thing, "Haydn, put the water on yourself and not on my clean floor."

The tub sat on a braided rug in front of the open oven of the stove, and a twelve-year-older had various techniques for bathing. If he weren't unduly large for his age, he could sit in the tub with his knees jackknifed under his chin. The quickest and perhaps the most efficient way was to stand up and work upward with handfuls of water. You spattered a good deal, but the rug was a large one and absorbed moisture well. Then you toweled off standing in front of the stove. Shep, our collie, was always on hand and insisted on licking a fellow's toes. It was an unhurried, pleasant process, and with the room to himself a lad didn't mind his bath too much.

It did seem a waste of time and effort in the winter to take a bath every week. After all, cold weather is different from warm weather; and besides, with a good heavy union suit, mighty little dirt got through to the skin. However, when it got along into the spring, and a boy could use the old swimming pool in the meadow, he and his Father agreed that two or even three baths a day were necessary. But a meadow swimming pool is different from a tin tub in a kitchen. I was definitely in favor of cleanliness if I could take my bath and a swim at the same time in cool water beneath overhanging willows.

Right after Saturday evening supper, Father got washed and dressed and then he said to me, "Haydn, why don't you see if Mother and the girls are about ready to go. And you might hitch Belle to the democrat while you're at it."

"Pa," I said, "can't we take the surrey?" That was a question I asked every Saturday evening, and Father's answer was always the same.

"Not this time, Haydn," he said. "The surrey is for special occasions."

I checked on the womenfolk and then went to the barn. As I hitched up the democrat, I cast a couple of longing looks in the direction of the surrey. It was my favorite means of transportation. There were buckboards and top buggies, democrats and broughams, one-horse farm wagons, stone boats, hayracks, and dump carts, but they were the everyday utilitarian vehicles. Each served its purpose; each was a sturdy plain affair that was designed for a specific job. The fringe-top surrey belonged in a different category. It was a luxury.

It often came to pass in the old days that some citizens by ability, hard work, and persistence accumulated enough to secure a few of the extras. And when it came to pass that a farmer had burned his mortgage, built up his herd and farm equipment, bought a nickel-trimmed parlor heater, a new carpet for the living room, and a parlor organ, he felt justified in buying a fringe-top surrey. A touch of luxury is good for a man, but a fringe-top surrey was a luxury the whole family could enjoy. It did something for a family's morale to ride in one of the snappy outfits to church, a Fourth of July picnic, and the Wednesday evening band concerts and political rallies.

It was an exciting day on the farm when Father announced that he guessed we could afford a surrey. The Acme Royal Canopy-Top Surrey cost $79.50, but you must expect to pay for style and prestige. The catalog description was enough to set a boy's imagination going, and when the surrey finally arrived I just couldn't believe my eyes. The long colorful tassels swayed gently; the upholstery was heavy wool, green English body cloth; the seats were full of springs and the backs were soft and comfortable to lean against. At each side of the front seat was a handsome, brass, imported, French, oil-burning lamp. The slender-tired wheels had narrow steel spokes. The front wheels were 38 inches high and the rear wheels 42. The body was hung on 1500-mile axles, with 36-inch elliptic end springs. The gear was hard-turned wrought iron. The body was painted a rich glowing green artistically striped with gleaming red lines. It weighed, crated for freight shipment, 825 pounds.

A fringe-top surrey gave a family standing in the community. A solid citizen did not purchase such a thing as a surrey until he could pay cash for it—and the community knew it. We were not the only family in Hancock that had one, but when it came to washing and polishing and taking care of it, we were second to none.

After I got Belle hitched up, Father and I usually had to wait a little longer for Mother and the girls.

"Never did understand what takes womenfolk so long to get ready," Father always said.

Finally Mother appeared with the eggs and butter she was going to barter at Fogg's General Store. The eggs were packed in a large green firkin with a woolen cover. There was a layer of sawdust on the bottom to prevent bumps that could cause a cracked egg. The pound prints of butter with the four-leaf-clover design on top were in another bucket, wrapped in newspapers to prevent them from softening in warm weather.

In due time the Pearson family loaded into the two-seated democrat and we started along the valley road to the village. Sometimes the neighbors above us came along about the same time; sometimes the neighbors between us and the village joined us on the way. It made quite a procession, but it posed a problem too. If you have ever lived on country roads you will remember the clouds of dust that swirled into the air as a wagon whirled by. Thus, in order to avoid the dust clouds, families had to space themselves out along the road. It was a sedate and dignified sight. When a couple of lads were driving to town and each had a fast-stepping roader, a little dust was a minor matter. Between Charles Sheldon's and the foot of Sand Hill there was a long level stretch, ideally suited for a brief horse race. But there was no racing when whole families were going to town.

Main Street Saturday night was a lively place. Families were there from all over the township. Fogg's General Store was filled; many persons made a visit to the library, and certain men, so I am told, visited the livery stable to test a liquid made from apples. We headed for Fogg's first

of all. Mother swapped eggs and butter for needed groceries. I took charge of getting the five-gallon can of kerosene filled and carried it back to the democrat. Father bought a few items and then joined the men around the stove. It made no difference if the stove was in use or not; men just naturally gravitated there to discuss crops, weather, and politics. There was much joking and laughter and a few tall stories told by unsmiling men. The ladies naturally gravitated around the notions counter and exchanged family news and gossip.

As for me, I just naturally gravitated toward the candy counter. I earned ten cents a week for doing the farm chores. Five cents was definitely allocated: two pennies for church, two for the Sunday School collection, and one for the penny bank. But that left a whole nickel, a very respectable sum of money, that I could spend at Fogg's. I went about it slowly, logically, and objectively.

The first step was to look through the curved glass front of the candy counter and debate with myself how to get the most value for my nickel. There was no hurry about it. I appreciated the fact that chocolates were delicious, but I also knew from experience that they had practically no lasting power. Besides there was always a fair chance that Father would buy half a pound of ice-cream drops for a family treat. Most Saturdays a penny stick of gum was a basic purchase, for a big stick of gum had long-lasting qualities if a fellow stuck the wad on his bedpost at night. That left four cents.

The choice was extensive. There were all-day suckers, candy cigarettes, coconut flags with red and white stripes, Boston baked beans, delicious sugar-coated peanuts in little pots, sticks of peppermint-flavored paraffin that were good chewing for a considerable time, generous-sized licorice sticks, candy plug tobacco with a shiny tin star pressed into the plug, Foxy Granpas, and Jackson Balls. I had to look over everything before I made up my mind: the Chewy Bagdads, Half Hours, Gibraltars, jawbreakers, Humbugs, Candy Buttons, Hokey Pokies, the little tin dishes full of hardened syrup, marshmallow bananas, and wafers with messages of tender affection, sour balls, and Cinnamon Imperials.

I usually bought a couple cents' worth of hard rock candies from among the many flavors: coltsfoot, ginger, horehound, wintergreen, birch, anise, sassafras, lime, clove, and molasses. That left two cents.

Now came the difficult part. I could either spend my two cents or save them for something special like a harmonica or a new fishing pole. I had a partiality for licorice sticks so I usually bought one of those, but more often than not I tucked that last penny in my pocket and felt pretty good about it.

After I bought my candy, my sisters started hanging around to see what they could get out of me. I got rid of them by going out on the store porch where the other boys were, playing mumblety-peg or Indian wrestling. They never followed me out there. They just stood by the door giggling and pretending not to notice us.

"Here comes Old Ben," one of the boys shouted. "Come on, let's follow him."

Old Ben wasn't one of the town's leading citizens. But he was dependable. Every evening he wheeled his old battered barrow along Main Street and lighted the street lamps that made fuzzy-edged, golden halos in the darkness.

Mothers did not worry when their boys followed Old Ben. In all the times that I followed him, I never heard him say anything out of line. Old Ben was a character, no question of that. He was the lamplighter for the village, the janitor of the village school, and the sexton of the tall-steepled white church that sat beside the village common.

Small fry were his faithful followers, and as he trundled his oversize barrow along he was accompanied by boys who listened wide-eyed to his stories. At each street lamp he went through the familiar ritual. He set a stubby, broken-topped, short ladder against the post and climbed up a couple of rungs. He took the kerosene lamps down to the barrow, filled the fount with kerosene, ran a black callused thumb over the burned wick to even it, pulled a stained dark cloth from his hip pocket and whisked it over the chimney.

Many a meticulous housewife exclaimed, "I declare, I don't see how Old Ben keeps those chimneys so clean with that dreadful-looking rag." Then he climbed the ladder and ran his cloth over the glass of the protecting cage. He lifted the lamp chimney, scratched a big kitchen match on his thumbnail, and touched it to the wick. He waited a few seconds to see that the flame burned evenly; then he closed the cage door, came down, put the ladder on the barrow, and accompanied by his retinue went along to the next street lamp.

Old Ben talked as he worked. No one knew too much about his early years, but he was the town's most traveled citizen. He had been all around the world on tramp freighters, he had worked in the cotton fields of Texas and had

226

followed grain harvests in the West. He had spent one or more winters in the logging camps of Oregon. He told us stories of far-off lands and described places and people in China, India, and South America. As he talked, names in our old dog-eared geography books suddenly came alive, and many a farm and village lad, listening to those tales of adventure, resolved that some day he too would see those distant lands.

Old Ben lived alone in a small three-room cottage at the edge of the village. His kitchen was spotlessly clean, the bedroom was always neat, and the little living room was filled with mementos of his travels. Maps on the walls almost covered the wallpaper. Sometimes on a Saturday morning boys gathered in his home and Old Ben pointed out the routes around the world that he had traveled. He spoke of memorable storms along the China coast and great snowfalls in Oregon. He pointed out places in South America where he had visited and worked.

You couldn't call Old Ben an important man—not in usual terms, but he served the town well and earned his living by faithful work. He was an old man when I first knew him and listened to his stories. But Old Ben was important to a group of boys. His tales of adventure opened vistas to young minds. His philosophy of life was solid. I can still hear him saying as we came to the last lamp by the Historical Society at the south end of the village street, "All right, boys, that's it for today. Now you hustle on back. Your folks are going to be wanting to start for home."

Saturday evening wasn't the only time we had a social outing. There always seemed to be something going on—a town meeting, a box supper, or a band concert. Naturally my sisters and I attended District School, and it was there that many of the village activities took place. The school was a humble utilitarian building located well back from the country road. Through that narrow front door trooped generations of boys and girls. They hung their coats and caps on a row of nails right by the door. At the battered, knife-carved desks they learned their lessons, and came forward to the settees at the head of the class to recite. The front entry from middle fall to late spring was always piled high with chunks of hardwood for the big round iron stove that stood at the front of the room. The stovepipe ran the length of the room and into the brick chimney at the rear; soot dropped from some of the joints of the metal pipe and made dark patches on the rough floor. In the back there were the two doors that led to the schoolyard—one for girls and one for boys.

Just inside the schoolhouse door was a shelf on which stood a pail of water with a tin dipper hanging from a nail above. In those days no one had heard of germs and so no one was afraid of the dipper. Getting the water was a privilege for one of the older boys. It meant a trip to the farmhouse just across the way, and Mrs. Johnson usually had a few cookies or a couple of hot doughnuts ready. A lad felt fairly safe in using twenty minutes for the trip, but sometimes he stretched it a bit too far. Teacher was likely to say, "Haydn, I know that pail of water is heavy and you have to stop to rest a few times. Still I think perhaps you are finding it a bit too much work. So we'll let John get the water next week." A boy took it with a grin; he knew Teacher was right. He had been spending just a bit too much time in Mrs. Johnson's kitchen or looking at the new colt in the Johnson barn.

Teacher's low platform and desk were in one corner; but she rarely was on the platform. She taught from the floor and could watch the big boys and girls in the back desks while hearing the fourth-graders give their lessons. Looking back over the years, I wonder how a teacher could teach all subjects in eight grades. But she did. And she taught well.

In those days it was taken for granted that boys and girls went to school to learn. They were supposed to master facts of history, geography, arithmetic, and English grammar, and if they didn't they heard about it. When they didn't keep up with their lessons, there would be no recess and a short noon hour for them. The penalties were stiff but fair. It was too much fun playing Indians or cops and robbers in the woods to take a chance of staying in at recess. School kept from nine to twelve and from one to four. It hurt to miss the mid-morning and mid-afternoon recesses; it was a real blow if Teacher said, "Abner, you take half an hour at noon and then spend the rest of the time doing those arithmetic examples." The noon hour was the highlight of the day, and to sit at a desk while the others were out playing or skating on the pond was a penalty that quickly taught a valuable lesson. As Teacher used to say, "Do your work well and get it out of the way and you'll enjoy your play time." And as a man looks back half a century, he wonders how many other life lessons he learned from the gentle-voiced but determined lady who taught so many years in District Six.

Unless it was a bitter cold day, we used to walk to school

with our lunch buckets in hand. Most of the children were up early to help with the farm chores, and a mile or two walk to school was a pleasant part of the day. A boy always had woodchuck holes to explore once the leaves were down in the fall, and after the first frost he could examine the hornets' nests. There was usually time to explore beneath the plank bridge or perhaps crawl along the rafters of a covered bridge. Sometimes walking to school was so pleasant that you didn't really mind when you finally got there.

The District School was often used as a center for many enjoyable village affairs, like Friday afternoon exercises, spelling bees, debates, and socials. When a box supper was announced, we knew we had a pleasant evening ahead. After noon recess on a Friday, Teacher would say, "Children, we're going to have a box supper tomorrow night, so the seventh and eighth grade boys will please give everything an extra good cleaning."

We knew what to do. First we swept the schoolroom and we were careful not to raise the dust. "Don't lift the broom, boys," Teacher admonished, "and you won't toss dust in the air." It was a fussy and slow task to do a real job of sweeping around the iron legs of the desks, and we knew from experience just how long to make the job last. Then we swept the entry, brought in wood from the shed behind the school and stacked it very carefully—and very slowly.

The larger girls dusted the schoolroom. Girls who were clever put colored chalk drawings on the blackboard. A string along the front held a row of crayon pictures that the little ones had drawn, and as I look back I think

Teacher was a practical psychologist, for everyone in the eight grades did something to help, or else had something on exhibition.

While we worked, Teacher rehearsed the pupils who would furnish the program after the boxes were auctioned off and the supper eaten. There were recitations and piano solos and piano duets. Sometimes we had a little one-act play. I was always ready to contribute a stirring rendition of "Horatius at the Bridge" or "The Wonderful One Hoss Shay."

On the appointed Friday the farm families in the district did the chores early and headed for the school and an evening's entertainment. I remember the happy spirit of good fellowship as the families arrived and the horses were blanketed and tied to the trees. I remember the fun and excitement as the boxes were auctioned off by Seth Woodward, our local auctioneer. He stood on the low platform that held Teacher's desk and thoroughly enjoyed himself as he egged on the bidders. Standard price was about a half dollar; but sometimes when two or three young squires wanted to eat with a certain girl, Seth would get a dollar for a box! It all helped to buy some needed equipment for the school.

The women prided themselves on home-cooked food, every box was a bargain, and there was lots of fun as some solid middle-aged farmer bid on a box from a lady and then announced in a loud voice that for once he was going to get a square meal. By seven o'clock or so, after everyone had had hearty meat sandwiches, cakes, pies, and cookies, we had the program. Fathers and mothers squeezed into desks they had used many years before; some sat on the settees at the back of the room and around the sides. Then we had the recitations and songs and music. Sometimes Father, as a member of the school committee, spelled down a group of parents, and it was fun for the children to see their parents fail on the same hard words that bothered them.

After the spelling bee, Seth Woodward usually led us in the singing, and it was about this time that some of the young men snuck out of the schoolroom for a stroll around the yard with the objects of their attention. At about nine o'clock folks rounded up their children and headed for home.

Every Friday afternoon at school we had what was called "Friday Afternoon Exercises." Teacher planned a little program of recitations, songs, piano pieces, and a spelling bee; and mothers and fathers used to drop in to see how their young ones were doing. When it came to the spelling bee, the bigger boys in the seventh and eighth grades usually did not shine. The trouble was the girls. It seems to me that girls are just naturally better spellers than boys, and my sister Mildred was the best of the lot.

I had one moment of glory, however. On a certain Friday there was a spelling bee, and Father, as a member of the school committee, was giving out the words. Father was a traditionalist; he believed in hard study; he expected children to know the answers to basic questions in history and geography. It wasn't considered old-fashioned to know the multiplication tables in those days. But Father was also a realist, and as we eighth-grade boys lined up on this particular occasion, neither he nor I had any rose-tinged expectations.

But Lady Luck rode with me; I went through several rounds and had the deep satisfaction of watching the other lads go back to their desks before I did. We sailed along. Sister Mildred and I kept our places. Usually Mildred and Mary Adams went down the stretch, battling it out for first place. Still I held on. The other boys were smiling; Teacher looked a bit surprised. I am sure Father and Mother were surprised.

Mildred and I were left. It was an unprecedented and unbelievable situation. "Iridescence" said Father. I'm sure Mildred gave me a pitying look as she sailed through it. She left out the first "c."

It was one of life's epochal moments. I took a breath and went to it. I did it. For years I have had to listen to Father's awed comment when I spelled that word correctly. "My gracious," he said. "He's done it."

The second Tuesday of March was a highlight of the year. District schools were closed. In pungs, sleighs, and on bobsleds behind plodding farm teams, everyone came to the tall white-spired meetinghouse on the village common. It was the day of the town meeting.

Horses were blanketed in the horse sheds behind the building. Men and women, boys and girls gathered in the meetinghouse, the lower floor of the big building. The moderator, town clerk, town treasurer, and the three selectmen sat in uncomfortable prominence on the stage. The big room was filled with wooden settees. Young fry scampered around the place and made frequent trips through the side door by the stage to the old-fashioned rest rooms. On either side of the entrance door, beside the steps that

led down the hall, was a huge wood-burning furnace—
and from time to time the janitor opened a door and tossed
in a four-foot hardwood log.

I remember the excitement of those meetings. I recall
the speeches made by men with whiskers and beards. Sometimes there were wordy battles, with the town divided into
two feuding clans; sometimes a selectman or a road agent
took a terrific lambasting from an irate citizen. I particularly remember Old Mose. He lived alone in a one-room
shack on a tolerably poor dirt road. His was the only habi-
tation on the road, and Old Mose never owned a team. In
the interest of economy, and there was deep interest in
the tax rate before rural America began to citify itself,
the road agent did not work on the road from spring to
fall. In the winter he went in with the snow roller and
his six-horse hitch so that Old Mose could make his Saturday night visit to the General Store.

But come town meeting we all knew what would happen. We would have been disappointed if Old Mose had
failed us. When it came to the article in the Town Warrant
which read, "To see if the town will raise and appropriate
the sum of $2,000 for roads, or take any action relating
thereto," it was the signal. Old Mose stood up. The moderator sat down, for he believed in democracy and bent over
backwards to give every citizen his say. Old Mose blasted
John Adams, the road agent; he blasted the newfangled era
with its electric lights and telephones. He condemned the
citizens of Hancock for partiality, and he quoted long passages by heart from the Constitution and Declaration of
Independence. One year Old Mose got carried away and
ended up with Lincoln's Gettysburg Address, and he re-

ceived a great hand when he finished in a blaze of oratorical glory.

There were arguments and counterarguments. Schools and roads were the main items of expense—even as they are today. At noon the Ladies' Sewing Circle served a dinner for 35 cents. At one o'clock the meeting began again. As it grew late, along about 3:00 to 3:30, farmers with cows to milk and chores to do began putting the articles through faster. And finally the moderator brought his gavel down with a bang and declared, "The meeting is adjourned."

Small towns have changed a good deal since then, but the town meeting has not outlived its usefulness. Nowadays small towns have budget committees and planning boards; the hard-top roads must be kept open in winter. In Hancock we never heard of such things, but I have never forgotten the basic principle that governs a town meeting. That principle is that in open meeting a man can say what he believes and vote as he wishes.

The highlight of the summer social season was the Wednesday evening band concert. Every week through July and August the Town Cornet Band gave a concert from the bandstand on the village common. Through the winter the band met periodically in the long upstairs room in the ell of Woodward's Hotel. Mr. Peavey, the director, knew what he wanted from his musicians, and by the time summer rolled around they were rehearsed to a fare-thee-well.

A band concert was an occasion, and I never had any trouble persuading Father to let me hitch up the fringe-top surrey. As seven o'clock drew near, farm families arrived from miles around. The village folks brought out

235

chairs, and an audience of three hundred or more made themselves comfortable around the common. The tall white church spire loomed overhead; the village school was across the common; the red brick vestry was across the street from the white circular bandstand with its green-shingled roof. There was a hush as Mr. Peavey lifted his baton, waited for a dramatic second, and then brought it down as the band struck up a stirring march.

The concert began in daylight and the band members, in snappy uniforms and caps that made them look like seagoing admirals, played favorite marches, familiar home songs, lilting waltzes, and gay polkas. After each number there was a wave of applause. Small boys were there in force. I can recall how the village constable wandered around and collared a few of the more rambunctious ones from time to time. His penalty was a sensible one. Boys had to sit on the ground in one spot for a few minutes where he could keep an eye on them. Then after two or three numbers they would be given their freedom—which sometimes did not last too long.

As dusk settled over the hills and valleys, lamps were lighted in the bandstand, and the shining reflectors behind the glass chimneys threw light for the musicians to read the music. Up and down the main street the street lamps made golden spots as the darkness deepened, looking like a line of beads on an invisible string. The concert lasted about an hour and a half, with a generous number of en-cores. In between numbers, men and women visited and got caught up on the news. Girls in white dresses and big hair ribbons wandered about sedately, pretending to ig-nore the boys.

Then came time for the final number. The band swung into "Good Night, Ladies," and from the throats of the audience came the familiar, beloved words. Into the warm night air the melody swelled—sweet high sopranos, rich altos, clear tenors, and strong basses. The band concert was over. Along peaceful country roads wagons wended homeward—and friendly stars twinkled over a little country town.

When winter came to Hancock, sleigh rides were the most important social event. I still remember those cold, brittle-air, star-studded nights when we piled onto a two-horse bobsled and drove to a neighboring town for an oyster stew supper. I remember the shafts of gray steam that shot from the horses' nostrils, and the bells on the collars that sent music into the night, harmonizing with that squeaking, dry, crunching noise as steel runners slid over the hard-packed snow.

I can't say that Old Charlie and Jerry were a pair of dashing steeds. They weren't the dashing type. They were faithful friends and we understood each other; but they were plodding and methodical. However, on a cold night they walked briskly, and on the downhill slants between Hancock and Peterborough they were willing to jog. I have always thought that Charlie and Jerry spent just as much energy and motion in bobbing up and down as they did in going ahead; but I also can truthfully say that they trotted toward home at a considerably faster pace than they went away from it.

A sleigh ride to Peterborough was the highlight of the winter. I don't want to start a controversy about sleds versus pungs. But in our region a two-sled vehicle was called a sled, while a pung had just one runner on each side. A sled was really two sets of sleds, and because the rear set was hitched to the front bob by a steel pin, it meant you could turn very sharply. We used our farm sled without the board bottom platform for hauling logs. When we hauled grain, ice, or sawdust, we put on the platform and the high board sides. This was the same outfit we used for the sleigh ride. Over the wooden platform we spread a layer of sweet-smelling timothy hay or oat straw. Over the hay went old quilts and horse blankets. There were buffalo robes and blankets to cover the folks on the ride.

Chores were finished early on the night of the ride. It

was about eight miles to the tavern in Peterborough. I don't pretend to remember exactly how long it took, but if memory serves somewhere near correctly, about eight o'clock we would be sitting down to a hot oyster stew. Charlie and Jerry were blanketed and in the warm livery stable behind the tavern.

Few young folks today know about such expeditions. As we left the farm with shouts and singing, a lantern fastened to a front stake, and the collar bells jingling, it seemed as if we were on a long jaunt. It was slow going up steep Putnam's Hill, and along the ridge to Adamses' and Fosters'. If I was handling the team, I wrapped the reins around a stake and joined the boys walking behind the sled. On a zeroish night, if Charlie and Jerry broke into a joggy trot down a little slope, we jogged along too. As we went by the farmhouses, we shouted and sang songs, and we would see Mrs. Adams and Mrs. Foster in the windows waving. Then we dropped down the hill to Johnson's Mill, and we were squared away for the six-mile run on nearly level ground into Peterborough.

A sleigh ride was fun all the way and you never knew what joke some lad would pull. I still recall the time we were coming home after our oyster stew and hot mince pie banquet. We had jogged along through the long level Swamp Woods, passed Johnson's Mill, and started up the long hill to the middle road that led home to Glenrose Farm. Most of the boys were walking behind the sled. Charlie and Jerry knew they were within a couple miles of home and were swinging along in good shape. It wasn't hard pulling on the slippery, hard-packed snow.

My friend Eddie was in the sleigh. Suddenly there were

239

screams and shouts, wails and shrieks. The girls threw off blankets and began tumbling from the sled. It was pandemonium. We knew Eddie or some other lad had pulled a stunt, but no one had an idea what had happened. All we knew was that when something of this sort occurred, there was a reason.

The girls were shouting and screaming at Eddie. It didn't bother the horses. Eddie was left alone standing in the sled. He walked toward the rear and he held his right hand out ahead of him. From it, dangling by its tail, was a good-sized mouse.

Eddie was pleased and so were we. I can still see him as he flipped the mouse away. Makes me think of the time someone put a mouse in the garbage pail at a Grange supper.

Christmas in Hancock was the best time of all. I had my doubts about Santa Claus, but it was common sense to stop teasing my sisters and to keep the wood box filled. No use taking chances if Santa required good conduct before he would leave that new knife a young citizen sorely needed.

It was strange, come to think of it. Every year without fail, Santa arrived in Hancock at precisely 7:30 in the evening, and he always came to the Town Hall. It has never been satisfactorily answered why Hancock was favored over Peterborough, Antrim, or Francestown. The Town Hall Christmas party was an annual event, and for weeks ahead Teacher had been rehearsing the children for their parts in the program. Little tots in the first grade had four-line poems; children in the fourth, fifth, and sixth grades had longer poems, and usually two talented girls played a piano duet.

It was a whole town party and everyone came. Some of the families were poor in this world's goods and some were comfortably well to do. It made no difference on Christmas Eve. It wasn't material things that counted; it was the night that Santa came to Hancock and the whole town came to see him. The Town Hall was crowded. The little children sat on the front settees, and behind them were half-grown men—twelve-year-olders like myself. Behind us, parents and friends filled the rest of the hall. On either side of the double door leading into the hall was a big wood-burning furnace. As you entered, the stage and its wings were to the left. Big brass-bowled hanging lamps shed a soft golden glow. It was just a small town Christmas party, but a high point of the year for everyone.

Father was chairman of the program committee and he saw to it that everything went on schedule. He gave a brief introductory talk and told us he had had communication with Santa and that everything was coming along on time. The program started and mothers' lips followed the words as little, pig-tailed girls struggled to get through their poems. Sometimes a little tot was overcome with the enormity of the situation and had to be rescued by a big sister; then the applause rang out twice as loud.

Each few minutes, between numbers, Father climbed the stage, went close to the big red brick chimney and cupped his ear up the flue. We all knew he was listening for the bells—the reindeer bells—that always sounded before Santa arrived. We watched Father's face, but all he did was to shake his head slightly from side to side. It was a tense atmosphere for the young ones on the front settees. Could it be that Santa had gone to another town?

241

Somehow we never noticed that Father disappeared. The last piano piece was played; the last poem was recited. Silence—deep, tense, hard-breathing silence settled in the hall. Then suddenly we heard them—heard the faint, distant, thin tinkling of the bells. Santa was coming! Santa was on time! No more need to worry. Santa had come from the North Pole, and somehow he had found Hancock.

The bells grew louder and louder. We heard the reindeers' hooves clatter and then Santa's deep resonant voice boomed out and carried over the hall: "Whoa there, Dasher, Dancer, and Prancer! Stand still, Vixen and Comet! Quiet, Cupid, Donder, and Blitzen!" There may be a few who don't believe in Santa Claus, but there are Hancock boys and girls scattered far and wide today who know that Santa is a real person. We saw him in those long ago days. We heard him talk and we had presents from his hand. He came down that chimney with a big pack. Some might think it strange that Santa knew all those boys and girls by name. Possibly it was more puzzling that he knew so much about the people of Hancock and their goings-on. For certainly Santa told jokes and recalled events that made the older folks laugh.

Then came the time for our presents, and Santa called the little ones to him and passed out those red net bags with a great big golden orange, a package of colored crayons, and a bag of ribbon candy. He talked to us a few minutes after the presents had been given out. I can't remember much of what he said. Probably he told us that Christmas was a holy day and that we celebrated the birth of Him who came to earth long years ago to point the way for men's feet. He probably said that peace on earth, good will to men seemed a long way from realization but that some day, somehow, men would learn to live together in peace.

Christmastime in the country was a different world. White beauty sparkled on the hills and upland ridges as the holiday drew near. For weeks before the Holy Day, each member of our family was busy and secretive, for most of the presents were handmade. On the afternoon of the day before Christmas, Mother would say, "Frank, you and Haydn get the tree and set it up, and after supper the girls and I will trim it."

It was an annual ritual on Glenrose Farm. With a light axe a man and his son climbed the orchard slope, went through the maple-sugar grove and among the evergreens above. Some years the sun was bright in a blue sky and the mountains across the valley were silhouetted against the pale horizon. There were years when the world was quiet and gray and you could feel the brooding expectancy as Earth waited for its white covering. It was peaceful among the spruces, hemlocks, and white pines. Chickadees came around and chanted cheerful alto songs; sometimes a partridge exploded from beneath a low branch; sometimes the hairy woodpeckers were drumming a roll call on dead boles.

We searched for the perfect tree—a seven-foot, symmetrical spruce with a strong top spike to hold the sparkling white star. When we found just the right one, we felled it carefully and took it back to the woodshed. Then it was set in a box that was used for this purpose each year, and carried into the living room.

We did the chores early on Christmas Eve; sisters redded

up the kitchen and then the family gathered in the living room. Shoeboxes filled with decorations came from the top shelf in the front hall closet. There were red paper bells that opened like accordions, shiny silvery metal balls, and red ornaments of various types. There were long strips of slender silvery tinsel and small gleaming white stars that fastened to branches. I remember the long strings of red cranberries, the strings of white popcorn, and the brown gingerbread men that hung from branch tips.

Father stood on a chair and fastened the big white star to the top spike. Then from hiding spots all over the house we brought out the presents. Small presents went on the branches of the tree; bulky ones were placed on the floor beneath it. It was exciting to see the presents pile up and to try to guess what might be in the packages.

Of course Christmas Day was a big event. A lad was up even earlier than usual and he was hoping against hope that something he wanted would be in the stocking that hung from the mantel behind the parlor heater. If a lad was in desperate need of a Barlow knife or a pair of red-topped, stylish arctics, it was reasonably certain that Santa had heeded his wishes. After breakfast and the chores were over, we gathered in the living room and my youngest sister passed around the presents. Mother always said, "Save the wrappings and ribbons, children."

But the memory that comes back most vividly is the picture in that farmhouse living room after the tree was trimmed on Christmas Eve. We gathered around the stove and watched the leaping red-orange flames paint pictures through the isinglass door. Father took his well-worn beloved Bible and read again the story of the Wise Men who followed a star across fields and hills to the manger in Bethlehem. Every year the story was as fresh and thrilling as before. Christmas meant presents and gifts and it meant a feast on Christmas day. But it also represented family love and unity and a nonquestioning sense of security that seems sadly lacking today.

Father would talk to us a few minutes after reading from the Bible. I do not remember his exact words, but as I took my hand lamp and climbed the steep stairs to my room, I thought about the true meaning of Christmas.

AFTERWORD

HE WAS sitting on a plank bench at the edge of the village common, looking at the mountain in the distance across the river valley. Perhaps he was seventy-five; perhaps he was eighty or eighty-five. It is difficult to tell the age of a retired hill-country farmer. He was long and lean, his face was leathery and deeply lined—the character lines that you see in old farmers who have lived intimately with New England's weather.

It was a warm brooding September afternoon and the old man sat motionless, enjoying the sun. His neat gray suit was a little too big around the shoulders and the sleeves were a bit too short. You could see his strong wrists that matched the large gnarled hands. He was alone and perhaps he was lonesome. I didn't know. You cannot tell for sure. A man with good thoughts always has enjoyable companions.

I sat down on the next bench and he turned, looked, and then smiled. I smiled in return, but it must have been five minutes before he spoke. "I was born over on that mountainside," he said. "Eighty-two years ago next month. Lived there all my life until last month. My daughter-in-law said I couldn't live there alone another winter. 'Wasn't logical,' she said. She's a good woman and takes good care of me. I like her and she has made my boy John a good wife. Guess she's right. It wouldn't be logical. Not much longer, anyway . . .

"Still, that's a mighty pretty place up there on the lower slope. See that white house and red barn and that line of sugar maples leading up from the road? My great-grandfather set out those trees the spring he was married. His wife Prudence was a great one for trees. Great-grandfather's father, Henry, settled there in 1792. He'd fought the English and the country gave him the farm. Some folks say Henry was foolish not to settle in the river valley. Better soil, they said. Near neighbors and town. But us Sanborns never needed towns. We wanted to be good neighbors and I guess we always was. Been town officials and church men. I was a selectman for twenty years. Been on the school committee for my district and was road agent for the mountain road for fifty years.

"But it was the farm that I hated to leave. City folks and town folks can't understand. Mustn't expect 'em to. They mean well. My daughter-in-law means well and I guess she's right. 'Tain't logical for a man my age to live up there alone. It will make a beautiful summer home for somebody.

"They say it is dangerous in the winter. I don't see anything dangerous about it. That's where I was born and all my ancestors. I know every foot of those 160 acres. Rough weather, a man don't need to go outdoors. Not if he's planned right. That's why we built long ells here in the

247

mountain country. Man can go from the kitchen to the woodshed, then along the wagon shed and toolshed right into a nice warm barn.

"You look like a city feller, mister, so you wouldn't know. But it's a mighty nice feeling on a bitter winter day, when it's down to zero and it's blowing a gale and the snow is drifting, to go into a warm barn and hear the horses whinny and the cows rattle their stanchions. Beautiful up there on the mountain after a snow storm. Those fields and pastures look as if they were covered with a white feather bed. You can see the village down here in the valley and the train coming along by the river. I always liked the sound of the whistle.

"I've ridden the snow roller over those roads in winter and plank-dragged 'em in the spring. Ever live on a mountain farm when spring comes to the northland? I ain't educated, mister, but you feel something inside when those open spaces turn green and the partridges are drumming in the woods.

"Maybe it was a little harder to farm those sidehill fields, but it's good soil and the Sanborns always treated it right. I've seen the time when fifty herd of cattle was tied up in that big barn and no Sanborn ever bought any hay or corn for his stock. I liked farming, mister. Began when I was fourteen. Only had six years of school, but I've read books and papers all my life. Don't see why learning and farming aren't about the best life there is.

"I've plowed those fields and planted corn and grains and potatoes. Haying is a wonderful time of year, and those fields gave big crops of timothy and clover if a man treated 'em right. See that orchard above the barn? I set out those Northern Spies, Pound Sweetings, and Russets for my bride.

"We had two sons, Mary and me. My older boy went to war in '14. He's sleeping over in France. Good boy, Robert was, and loved to farm. He was all Sanborn. Planned to marry Jenny when he came back. My wife died in '19. Always thought her heart never healed after Robert went.

"John is a good son, but he wasn't meant to farm. My daughter-in-law is good. She says it isn't logical for me to live alone any longer. But after eighty-two years, the farm . . . has sort of become part of me. But I guess it wouldn't be logical to live there any more."

On my way home that afternoon, I thought about what the old man said. He was right, I guess. New Hampshire isn't logical, but once you've tasted the flavor of the New Hampshire countryside, you'll remember it for the rest of your life.

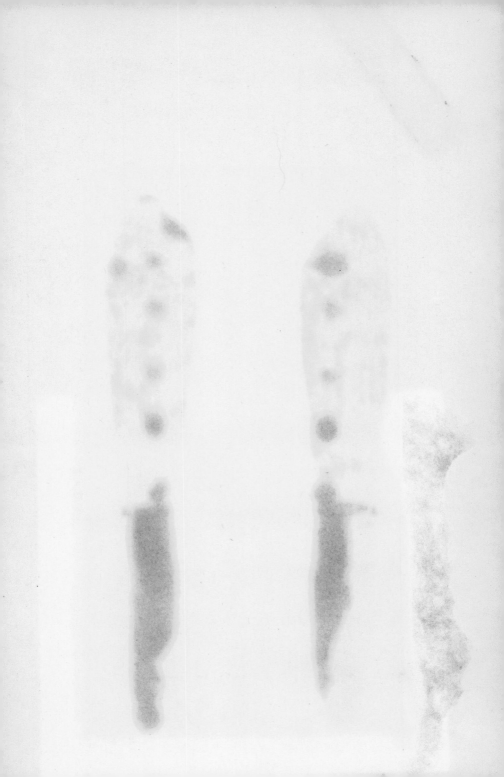